TY

By the staff of Editions Berlitz

 Library of Congress Catalog Card No. 84-080151.
Printed in Switzerland by Weber S.A., Bienne.

2nd Printing
1985/1986 Edition

How to use our guide

- All the practical information, hints and tips that you will need before and during the trip start on page 104, with a complete rundown of contents on page 107.
- For general background, see the sections Tyrol and the Tyroleans, p. 6, and A Brief History, p. 12.
- All the sights to see are listed between pages 28 and 88. Our own choice of sights most highly recommended is pin-pointed by the Berlitz traveller symbol.
- Entertainment, nightlife and other leisure activities are described between pages 89 and 97, while information on restaurants and cuisine is to be found on pages 98 to 103.
- Finally, there is an index at the back of the book, pp. 127–128.

Although we make every effort to ensure the accuracy of all the information in this book, changes occur incessantly. We cannot therefore take responsibility for facts, prices, addresses and circumstances in general that are constantly subject to alteration. Our guides are updated on a regular basis as we reprint, and we are always grateful to readers who let us know of any errors, changes or serious omissions they come across.

Text: Jack Altman
Photography: Jürg Donatsch
Layout: Doris Haldemann
We're particularly grateful to Dr. Hubert Gundolf of the Tyrol Tourist Office and Dr. Hans Timko of the Austrian National Tourist Office for their help with the preparation of this book.
Cartography: Falk-Verlag, Hamburg.

Contents

Maps

Tyrol and the Tyroleans

The Tyrol used to be a place people went to on their way to somewhere else. Now they stop—not only in winter for some of the finest skiing in the world, but also in summer. To wander among craggy mountains, across green alpine meadows, while streams rush down to sleepy valleys where a sturdy bunch of people serve excellent food and some pretty good wine. With, if you're lucky, a yodel and a jolly little thigh-slapping dance thrown in for good measure.

The Tyrolean Alps stand between Northern Europe and Italy. This gave the region a head start in the tourism industry. Over the centuries, more and more inn-keepers were needed to cater for Catholic pilgrims on their way to Rome, for Italian merchants seeking

out the lucrative markets of Germany or the Netherlands, as well as for journeymen artisans going in both directions and massive armies whose officers demanded more comfortable billeting than mere field camp, however picturesque. So if you find the hoteliers and local tourist office staff much more efficient than Austria's easy-going national reputation might have led you to expect, it's because they've been in the business a few centuries longer than anyone else.

The land they offer for your enjoyment consists of two spectacular tiers of mountains —the Lechtaler Alps, Karwendel and Kaisergebirge ranges along the Bavarian border in the north and the Ötztaler, Zillertaler and Deferegger Alps along the Italian border in the

Every Tyrol home has flowers, and the younger generation's still happy to wear traditional dress.

south. Separating the two tiers is the valley of the fast-flowing River Inn, silver-grey when the mountain snows are thawing, but in high summer a green as deep as the legendary blue of the Danube.

Except for the Lech (which flows into the Danube), all of Tyrol's many rushing rivers pour into the Inn. At its first historic bridge is the Tyrolean capital, Innsbruck, former home of Habsburg dukes and princes, today the thriving point of departure for summer tours of the province and a natural host for the Winter Olympics (1964 and 1976). International sport on the skiing slopes has brought fame to such resorts as Kitzbühel and St. Anton, but for the summer visitor these towns must compete with the charms of Mayrhofen or Fügen in the Zillertal, Serfaus or Lermoos and Ehrwald in the foothills of the Zugspitze (Germany's highest mountain), Rattenberg in the Inn valley and Alpbach in the Kitzbüheler Alps, St. Johann on the edge of the Kaisergebirge and the pretty little villages around Lienz in East Tyrol.

The region's small towns—even the largest, Innsbruck, has a population of only 122,000—boast exquisite Baroque churches, the meticulously maintained traditional architecture of houses and inns, and fascinating folk art. But the essence of the Tyrol is to be found in its mountains and rivers, in the valleys beyond the towns. You'll revel in the pure air, gentle by day, exhilaratingly crisp in the evening, and the clear, clear light, making the greens and blues a little greener and bluer than you may be accustomed to in the quiet of the forest and the refreshing sparkle of the mountain streams. All this is to be discovered in walks you take at your own speed, relaxed or vigorous, as you choose, with plenty of pauses to contemplate the beauty and to have a snack and a siesta in the shade. Or even a swim in the surprisingly warm waters of mountain lakes (a phenomenon of this alpine marshland, the geographers say).

So rather than making your holiday target a town, though one resort or another can always serve as a kind of (very comfortable) base, think in terms of one or more of the val-

The Bschlaber Tal's tranquillity in the gentle, late afternoon sun.

leys into which the Tyrol conveniently divides. To name only a few of the better known valleys, from west to east, you can choose among the Lechtal (*Tal* = valley), running south-west from Reutte, the Ötztal, the Stubaital south of Innsbruck, the Zillertal, the Wildschönau, the Felbertauern or Pustertal of East Tyrol. With a car you can explore the side valleys and tour the high mountain roads. But always be ready to get out and walk. The hinterland offers endless discoveries.

The province is Austria's third largest but the sparsest in population, its half-million or so inhabitants scattered only 29 to the square mile (47 to the square kilometre). Some smart manoeuvring by Italy at the end of World War I lopped off South Tyrol, more than half of the pre-1914 province. This left the principal part of the Tyrol separated from its eastern portion by a wedge of the province of Salzburg.

But the machinations of international diplomacy have done nothing to weaken the regional pride of the Tyroleans. However patriotically Austrian, they seem to feel themselves a people apart, with special local traditions, distinctive costume and a dialect you could cut with a knife.

The binding force of their lives is the Catholic religion. In a country where Protestantism made negligible inroads, the Tyrol has maintained the strongest front against the assault of reform and scepticism. This *heiliges Land Tirol* (Holy Land of Tyrol), as it is known in the German-speaking world, is dotted with wayside chapels and carved wooden crosses *(Wiesenkreuz)*. In almost every private home and public hostelry, a corner marked by a crucifix is set aside for prayer. As you travel through the countryside, you'll see the ubiquitous red slate or wooden-tiled steeple or bulb dome of the parish church (except in the Zillertal, a valley ceded in the 19th century by Salzburg to the Tyrol, where steeples and domes on the eastern slopes are painted a distinctive Salzburg green). Tyroleans adore religious processions. They never miss an opportunity in the Catholic calendar, whether Palm Sunday, Easter, Corpus Christi, Assumption or, of course, Christmas, to dress up in costume and parade through town behind a statue of Jesus, Mary or a patron saint.

But you'll also see the *Tracht,* as the costume is known, as everyday wear: knee breeches, short loden jacket

Time-honoured techniques work well enough for the Tyroleans.

and small green hat for men; white blouse and dark dress or skirt covered by a blue apron for the women, with a bonnet and neckerchief. Traditions are still sacred but worn lightly.

As modern as facilities for visitors may be, the Tyrol is a conservative region where customs and attitudes are still very much dictated by the tillers of the soil. The province has not escaped the urbanizing and industrial trends of the 20th century: today only 10 per cent of the working population is actively involved in farming or forestry. Nonetheless, the Tyrol is pervaded by its historic rural culture. In the popular imagination, the peasant remains the dominant Tyrolean figure. For him leather breeches are a work uniform, not a quaint vestige of a vanished past. His farm is still the most characteristic feature of the landscape, and for all his reliance on modern technology, he still lugs hay down the steep alpine slopes in huge sheet-bags hoisted on his back. And peasant cooking—"cuisine" would be too effete a word for the fine, robust fare served up piping hot from iron pans—sets the tone for the best restaurants of Innsbruck or Kitzbühel, as it does for the little village *Gasthof* that awaits you at the end of that long walk.

Despite a powerful sense of Tyrolean solidarity, there is no easily identifiable Tyrolean character or temperament. Moods seem to change from one valley to the next—open and friendly here, cool and reserved just over the hill. No anthropologist or social psychologist has yet established a direct correlation, but you may as a visitor notice that the inhabitants in the gently curved, U-shaped valleys tend to be of a more cheerful disposition than those in the steeply sloped, V-shaped valleys. Maybe it has something to do with the amount of sun they get. Some people claim it's because the yodel in a V-shaped valley sounds like a melancholy wail—while a U-shaped yodel is a whoop of joy.

A Brief History

The earliest artefacts uncovered by archaeologists provide indicators for Tyrol's subsequent importance in the German empire, in Napoleon's conquest of Europe and in the great wars of our own century. Bone spearheads found near Kufstein on the north-east border with Germany date the Tyrol's first human settlement to the Old Stone Age; in the same area excavators also unearthed traces of a bronze foundry of 1500 B.C. This was the forerunner of the great silver- and copper-mining industry established in the Middle Ages at nearby Schwaz—a major source of revenue for the German emperors.

By the 8th century B.C., Tyrol's alpine passes had become thoroughfares for the transporting of Greek and Etruscan goods from north and central Italy to the eastern Alps and northern Europe. The Romans took command of these strategically vital routes, and by A.D. 50 Emperor Claudius had incorporated the Tyrol into the province of Rhaetia, ruled from Augsburg. There were only two urban settlements in the Tyrolean Alps—Trento (Tridentinum) in the south and

Aguntum, remains of which can be seen today just outside Lienz in East Tyrol.

What began as a mere link in the lines of communication with the empire's northern and eastern territories became a bastion against mounting Germanic invasions—as it was later for the Habsburgs in their struggle against Napoleon. A major Roman military base was built in the 4th century A.D. at Wilten (Veldidena), today a suburb of Innsbruck. The Roman defences crumbled, Aguntum was abandoned, and in 550, the Franks took over. The Romanized population had converted to Christianity—as testified by relics of a 5th-century basilica at Lavant—but neighbouring communities were concurrently performing acts of human sacrifice to the god Saturn.

Over the next three centuries, the region was up for grabs, invaded by Lombards from the south, Slavs from the east and Bavarians from the north. Pursuing a policy that was to become the classical pattern for European colonialism, the Bavarians established monasteries in the wake of conquest, from which to convert the Slavs to Christianity and win their hearts and minds for the German empire.

Imperial Pawn

The Bavarians smoothed the way for Charlemagne to incorporate the Tyrol into his empire in 788. Under his sons and grandsons, the region was divided up again into a Bavarian north, Italian south and Carinthian-Slavonic east, with German culture playing an increasingly dominant role.

To counter the ambitions of aggressive nobles in the 11th and 12th centuries, the emperors formally placed the lands and temporal powers of the Tyrol in the hands of bishops ruling from Freising and Regensburg in Bavaria, from Salzburg, and from Trento and Bressanone (Brixen)* in Italy. But in practice the church had to entrust its holdings to the local aristocracy in exchange for military protection, while retaining control of silver and salt mines, mills, customs duties, trade, the minting of coins and the judiciary. Eventually the precarious balance of power between church and nobles shifted in favour of the latter as Count Albert III successively moved to unify the

*Throughout the text, Italian names are used for towns now under Italian government, with the German names in brackets only when substantially different.

Tyrolean territories through political and marital alliances.

In the 13th century the consolidation process was completed by Count Meinhard II, who emerged as the ruler of an area stretching from the Zillertal in the north to the River Avisio in the south, from the Lechtal in the west to the River Rienza in the east. The territory was for the first time given the name Tyrol, derived from the title of Meinhard's castle near Merano. To bolster his power, Meinhard turned to the church, designating the abbey of Stams (founded by his wife in 1273) as a major religious centre and the burial place for his dynasty.

The establishment of the Cistercian order there was at the time of only secondary importance. And for further support he looked to the Habsburgs, supporting Rudolf in his war against the Bohemian King Ottokar.

The first half of the 14th century was a difficult time for the Tyrol. Plagues of locusts destroyed the crops, earthquake devastated the villages and the bubonic plague decimated the population. On top of that the region became a focus for dynastic struggles between the Habsburgs and the Bavarian Wittelsbachs. By 1342 the Wittelsbachs were in command, granting Tyrol a kind of Magna Charta *(Grosser Freiheitsbrief)* which nonetheless left Bavarians in key administrative positions. Meinhard II's granddaughter Margarethe thought she could get better terms from the Habsburgs. In 1363 the Austrian rulers agreed to protect the Tyrol in exchange for control of the strategic north-south trade routes through the region, as well as communication links with the western territories of the German empire.

Unlike the absentee Wittelsbachs, the Habsburg dukes flattered the Tyroleans by coming to live in their region: Friedrich IV established his residence at Innsbruck in 1420. In addition, the peasants were given hereditary rights to lands they worked for overlords.

The wayside cross is a common feature of piously Catholic Tyrol.

Letting the Good Times Roll

Friedrich, who commanded the respect of his subjects because he sided with the peasants against the nobles, was known as the fellow "with the empty purse" since he was said to be constantly without cash. But the Tyrolean economy was in fact on the upswing after the disasters of the previous century. From 1420 on, silver mining in Schwaz proved increasingly lucrative. Pioneers in organized pressure for higher wages, more progressive labour laws and social welfare, the Schwaz miners made up the useful nucleus of an army whenever necessary. Salt mining around Hall also provided steady revenues. The travel trade was boosted when the Pope increasingly encouraged pilgrimages to Rome. German students, mercenaries, miners and printers were journeying south. Italian doctors, apothecaries and money-lenders were going north. They all used the Brenner and Reschen passes, and the inn-keepers reaped the benefits.

Duke Sigmund (ruled 1439–1490) moved the mint from Merano to Hall, to have the money nearer the Schwaz mines and his Innsbruck residence. But he spent it faster than it came in. He bought costly artworks and squandered a fortune on his great passion for hunting, providing elaborate harnessing and leatherware for his horses and huntsmen and building luxury lodges all over the Alps—lodges named *Sigmundskron, Sigmundslust* and, yes, *Sigmundsfreud*. Hunting was not his only passion. He fathered 40 bastards, but not a single legitimate heir. Finally he asked the Bavarian Duke Albrecht to pay off his debts in exchange for control over Tyrolean lands. But Maximilian, son of Habsburg Emperor Friedrich III, stepped in to pension off his crazy cousin and take over the reins of government in 1490. Sigmund was allowed to go on hunting and fishing wherever he liked.

Soon to become German emperor, Maximilian (Archduke of Tyrol 1490–1519) was without doubt the most notable of Tyrol's rulers. A man of great vision—with enormous personal ambition to match it—he sought to expand his empire into France, Italy and Hungary. He displayed the coats-of-arms of his actual and projected acquisitions on the grand façade of the *Goldenes Dachl* in Innsbruck (see p. 35). His successes more often came from the time-honoured Habsburg practice of judicious mar-

A brass band plays in the loggia of Maximilian's Goldenes Dachl.

ital alliances, both his own and his close kinsmen's, than from military conquest. So it was that he married Marie of Burgundy and then Bianca Maria Sforza of Lombardy. For all his continental preoccupations, he never forgot his residence in the Tyrol. The local silver and copper mines came in handy when funds were required to finance expensive projects. "Tyrol", he said with great affection, "is a money bag from which you never come away empty-handed".

The richness of the region's copper deposits led Maximilian to found a new arsenal in Innsbruck. Though he preferred quiet negotiations to battle, as in the peaceful acquisition of the east Tyrolean territories of Lienz, Kals, Virgen and the

Pustertal, heavy artillery from the Innsbruck arsenal proved useful in the 1504 campaign to wrest Rattenberg, Kufstein and Kitzbühel from the house of Pfälzer.

Maximilian flattered Tyrolean pride by granting the region special military status and according its people the right to bear arms for territorial defence. Less popular was Maximilian's demand for higher taxes to pay for his expansionist dreams. After Innsbruck innkeepers flatly refused credit to the emperor's retinue when he had left too many bills unpaid, Maximilian reneged on his plan to be buried in a monumental tomb in the Tyrolean capital's court church, the Hofkirche. In defiance of the imperial testament, his successor as ruler of the Tyrol, grandson Ferdinand, set up the magnificent monument in the Hofkirche. To this day, dozens of statues stand in attendance on an empty grave. Maximilian's body remained at Wiener Neustadt.

Countering the Reformation

But that was not enough to make the very conservative, Spanish-educated Ferdinand popular with the Tyroleans. They had become restless under the influence of the Lutheran Reformation and the Peasants' Revolt in Germany in the 1520s. The discontent was less a questioning of Catholic orthodoxy than a quest, as so often in their history, for greater regional autonomy. The miners of Schwaz and Hall demanded reforms. In southern Tyrol, Michael Gaissmair led a peasant uprising which was both revolutionary—calling for reforms in health, child care and welfare—and authoritarian, xenophobic, even anti-Semitic—out of hostility to Ferdinand's chief counsellor and treasurer, Gabriel de Salamanca, a converted Jew. Gaissmair sought an alliance with Swiss Reformer Ulrich Zwingli in Zurich and help from France and Venice. But most of the peasants marching from Salzburg to the Pustertal in 1526 were driven out of the Tyrol into Venetian territory. Thereafter, all deviation from the established Catholic order, such as isolated groups of Baptists attempted over the next few years, was violently repressed.

Archduke Ferdinand II was more popular than his father; he cut a romantic figure, marrying the beautiful and cultivated commoner Philippine Welser, daughter of a rich Augsburg merchant, against the wishes of the church and his fellow Habsburgs. The royal couple actually had to pretend their two sons were foundlings. The archduke gave his wife the charming castle of Ambras overlooking Innsbruck, assembling there a rich art collection and library.

Despite his broad culture, Ferdinand II proved a strict censor of books perceived as a threat to the Catholic establishment. The Counter-Reformation was pursued with great vigour in the Tyrol. In the 1560s the Jesuits, and then the Franciscans, were brought to Innsbruck to supervise proper observation of Catholic orthodoxy. Liturgy and ritual were given a more elevated tone, disdaining reformist calls for greater simplicity. This went down very well with peasants and patricians alike, both more conservative than their counterparts elsewhere in the German-speaking world. It was at this time that the Tyrol gained its name of *heiliges Land* (holy land).

Apart from some skirmishes and plundering in the north-east around Reutte and in the Lechtal in 1632, the Tyrol managed to stay out of the bloody Thirty Years' War; nevertheless, the economy suffered. Schwaz's mining heyday had passed with the 16th century. The costs of draining off underground water had proved greater than ore revenues, and the competition from Spain's new colonies in South America was just too tough. By 1660 those German financial investors, the Fuggers and Baumgartners, pulled out and Tyrolean miners took their expertise to Bohemia, Hungary, Italy, Spain, England, Russia—even to Venezuela.

Vienna Takes Over

In 1665 Archduke Sigmund Franz died without heirs, leaving Tyrol in the hands of a Vienna-based Habsburg, Leopold I. This effectively ended Tyrolean autonomy. In the realm of taxation, for instance, Tyrol's representatives could negotiate only on the amount to be levied, not on whether a tax was to be imposed.

The War of Spanish Succession at the turn of the 18th century showed just how fierce local patriotism could be. At first, Tyrol served only as a corridor for troop movements. The Bavarian Elector Prince Max Emanuel occupied Innsbruck in 1703. Austria's imperial troops did not react and it was Tyrol's own militia, acting on that special military mandate conferred by Maximilian 200 years earlier, which drove the Bavarians out. The victory, on July 26, St. Anne's Day, is commemorated by the Annasäule (Ann's Column) in Innsbruck.

Tyrol's subordination to Vienna was formalized by Empress Maria Theresa in 1749. It meant accepting "foreign-born" governors, such as Count Johann Gottfried von Heister from neighbouring Carinthia. Once again, an attempt was made to soothe Tyrolean ire: in 1765 Maria Theresa decided to celebrate the wedding of her son Leopold in Innsbruck. A triumphal arch was specially built, but the death of her husband Franz meant a last-minute cancellation.

The ideals of the Age of Enlightenment were met with hostility in Tyrol. People here opposed the idealistic reforms of Emperor Joseph II: the establishment of new high schools to counter Jesuit influence, the closing down of "superfluous" monasteries, *i.e.* those devoted purely to religious meditation rather than practical works. Most of all, they were hostile to his charter of 1781 *(Toleranzpatent),* which allowed for the formal establishment of major religious congregations other than Roman Catholic.

After Joseph died in 1790, Tyrol's civic leaders took their cue from the French Revolution to urge the convening of their parliament *(Landtag).* But far from wanting to propose revolutionary new ideas, the Tyroleans brought 2,000 complaints and requests for the overthrow of Joseph's progressive reforms. In particular, "for the upholding of morality and religion", they called for an end to the Toleranzpatent. Joseph's reactionary successors, first Leopold II and then Franz II, were more than happy to oblige.

With the clamour of revolution drawing ever nearer, Franz II imposed strict censorship and police controls, with the blessing of the majority of Tyroleans. In 1796 and 1797, Bonaparte's army was on Tyrol's southern frontier. The French refused to recognize the Tyrolean militia as regular soldiers and summarily shot them whenever captured. They briefly occupied Bolzano and Bressanone, but withdrew prior to the peace treaty of Campoformido. The Coalition Wars of 1799–1805 brought the French back to Tyrol, to the western alpine pass at Nauders and the north-west Ausserfern region around Reutte. But the province's status was not affected until Bonaparte had become Emperor Napoleon.

Resistance

Under terms of the Peace of Pressburg following Napoleon's victory over the Austrians at Austerlitz in 1805, the emperor handed Tyrol to his Bavarian allies. During the Napoleonic occupation the region was renamed South Bavaria, a supreme humiliation. The Bavarians imposed severe anticlerical measures, expelling the Jesuits and confiscating church property and art treasures. They exercised an oppressive military control that finally provoked open resistance in 1809.

As Archduke Karl's Austrian army exerted pressure from Carinthia and the Pustertal, revolt broke out, heroically led by Andreas Hofer, from an inn-keeping family of San Leonardo in the southern Tyrol. Hofer, who had been a delegate to the 1790 Landtag in Innsbruck and had led the militia against the French in 1796, was a brilliant, charismatic personality enormously popular among the influential innkeepers of Tyrol. He was also in constant contact with Archduke Johann, ardent champion of Tyrol's cause at the court in Vienna. Once again, the local

A Vespa leaves no doubt: Merano is well and truly part of Italy.

militia were left to fight alone after the Austrian armies withdrew to face Napoleon. In May 1809, Hofer's men scored a notable victory at Bergisel, forcing the Bavarians to evacuate Innsbruck.

But the subsequent French success over the Austrians at Wagram, outside Vienna, led to the reoccupation of Tyrol by Napoleonic forces, this time under Marshal François Lefèbvre. Encouraged by renewed support from southern Tyrol, Hofer continued to fight against France's allies, the Bavarians and Saxons, around Lienz, along the River Adige (Etsch) and at Landeck. Another fine victory at Bergisel in August drove the French out of Innsbruck and Hofer became the governor of Tyrol.

But yet again, Austrian military and diplomatic subjugation to Napoleon vitiated Tyrol's hard-won triumphs, this time by terms of the October Treaty of Schönbrunn. Besides returning the northern portion of the province to the Bavarians (who incorporated the Zillertal from the province of Salzburg), Napoleon fatefully handed the southern half over to his Italian vassals. With Italian its official language, it became *Dipartimento Alto Adige* and Italian intellectuals celebrated this "reunion with the motherland", a "reunion" that would be definitively consecrated a century later in 1919 by an independent Italy.

Meanwhile, against overwhelming odds, Hofer was again urged by radical nationalists to continue resistance; but after initial victories at Merano and in his home territory of Val Passiria (Passeiertal), Hofer's forces were crushed in eastern Tyrol. He himself was betrayed and captured in January 1810. Fearing the threat of this already legendary hero at the head of some future Tyrolean separatist movement, the Austrian Emperor Franz II made no attempt to intercede for his life and Hofer was executed at Mantua.

With the same thought in mind after Napoleon's defeat, Chancellor Metternich was quick to counter Archduke Johann's reported plans to set himself up as an independent monarch at the head of a new Tyrolean uprising. It was forbidden to commemorate the 1809 resistance, and Hofer's remains had to be transferred to Tyrol clandestinely. He was interred in the Innsbruck Hofkirche against Vienna's wishes. A monument to the hero was not erected until 1838.

Back to Normal

Returned to Austria by the Congress of Vienna (1815), the Tyrol was confirmed in its historical conservatism. The province's liberals, always in a minority, had to publish their polemics in south German newspapers because of Austrian press censorship.

In spite of the national reintroduction of Joseph's Toleranzpatent, conservative-clerical resistance from Innsbruck prevented Protestants in the Zillertal from establishing a congregation in 1832. Some 400 of them were obliged to emigrate to Prussian Silesia. (The Tyrol, in fact, delayed recognition of non-Catholic schools and congregations until 1892.) In 1838 the Jesuits returned in triumph to Innsbruck, and the Tyrolean capital offered an ideal refuge for Emperor Ferdinand when he fled Vienna during the revolution of May 1848.

Socialism, not surprisingly, made little headway. A Social Democratic Party was founded in Tyrol in 1890, but was always hampered by the lack of an industrial proletariat. Support came from minorities in Innsbruck, Wörgl and Lienz, Bolzano and Merano, and from some railway workers.

Towards the close of the century, the Italian-speaking population pressed harder for more equitable treatment. They wanted the administration to accept Italian as an official language, but above all they called for greater parliamentary representation: against seven Italian-speaking deputies for 40 per cent of the inhabitants were the German-speaking population's 45 deputies for their 60 per cent. Nationalist Giuseppe Mazzini explicitly demanded that Italy's northern frontier be drawn at Tyrol's alpine passes (Reschen, Timmelsjoch, Brenner and the Pustertal). Vienna tried to placate the Italians by opening an Italian law faculty at the University of Innsbruck in 1904. But Pan-German nationalists rioted and the faculty was closed down.

Tyroleans responded with great patriotism at the outbreak of World War I, sending troops off to fight in Polish Galicia and Serbia; but heavy losses soon dampened local enthusiasm for the cause. By January 1918, demonstrations and strikes broke out under the leadership of the Social Democrats. A month later, Tyrol was directly touched by the fighting for the first time when Italian aircraft bombed Bolzano and Innsbruck.

Italy remained neutral until

April 1915, when a secret treaty promised them territorial gains, including South Tyrol to the Reschen and Brenner passes, if they entered on the side of the British and French. The promise was kept with the Treaty of Saint-Germain-en-Laye (May 1919). South Tyrol—or Alto Adige, as it was to be known—was handed over to Italy. Faced with the prospect of a future union between Germany and Austria, Italy regarded this acquisition as essential to its military security—an act, as Italian Prime Minister Antonio Salandra himself put it, of "sacro egoismo". Combined with Trentino, which had also once been under Austrian administration, though almost entirely Italian-speaking, the new province now numbered 290,000 Italian- and 220,000 German-speaking inhabitants (plus a small Ladino minority).

Dealing with Hitler—and Peace

The disillusionment arising from the debacle of World War I led inexorably to further disaster in the 1930s. The postwar provincial government was dominated two-to-one by the clerical-conservatives of the Tiroler Volkspartei (Tyrolean People's Party). Amid the

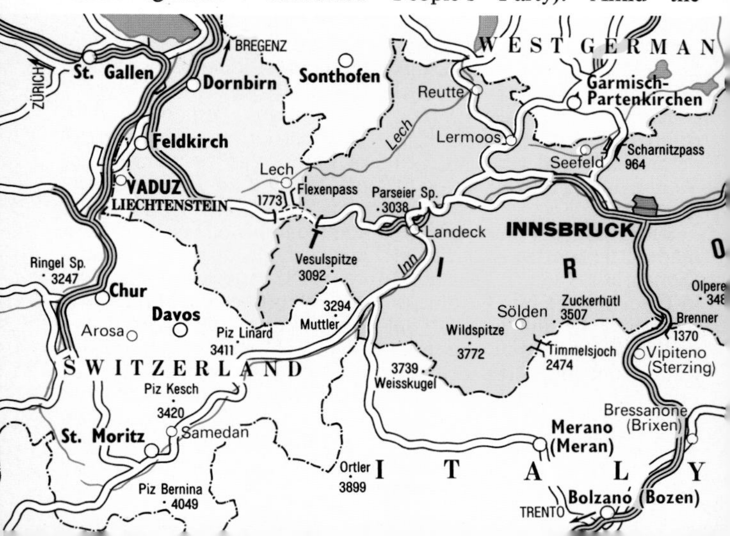

cacophony of competing nationalisms, it invoked a plague on all their houses and pressed for an independent state of Tyrol. The Social Democratic and Liberal opposition wanted to join with Germany. A groundswell of support for the idea won over the Tiroler Volkspartei and by 1921 the people voted 98.5 per cent for unification with Germany.

In the hysteria of the times, paramilitary groups sprang up to combat the kind of revolution that had triumphed briefly in Munich and Berlin in 1919. The strongest was the anti-Marxist Home Guard *(Tiroler Heimatwehr),* led by Prussian Major Waldemar Probst, who had killed the communist leaders Rosa Luxemburg and Karl Liebknecht in Berlin. In 1927, the guard crushed a strike of transport workers. Forgetting the scars of South Tyrol, it accepted support from the Italian Fascists when forming a political party for the 1930 national elections. This was soon followed by an alliance with Germany's Nazis.

In local elections in April 1933, three months after Hitler's accession to power, the Tyrolean branch of the Nazi Party won 41.2 per cent of the vote. The Austrian government outlawed the Nazis in June, but

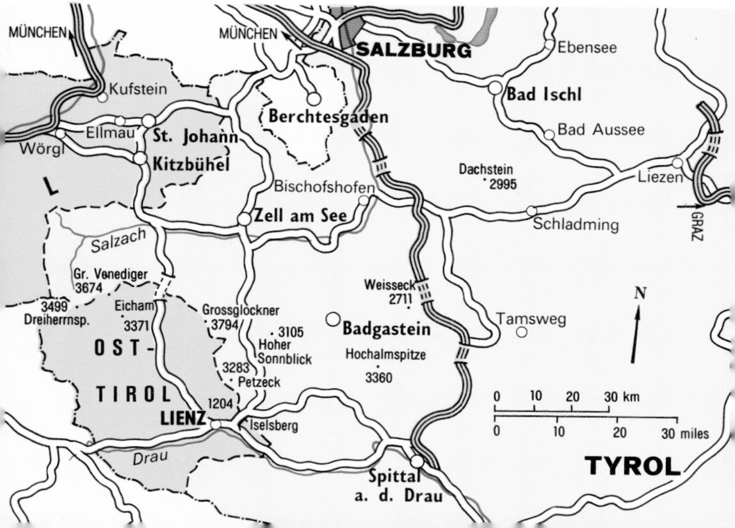

party members formed an Austrian Legion on the Bavarian-Tyrolean frontier. Over the next five years, Tyrol's tourist trade suffered greatly from German restrictions on foreign travel, and people looked enviously at the Nazi's economic successes, especially in overcoming unemployment.

Tyrol was more than ready for the "Anschluss" of March 1938. When the German Wehrmacht rolled across the Tyrolean border at Scharnitz and Kufstein, they were greeted by exuberant crowds—in those early days still spontaneous—shouting "Sieg Heil!" and waving swastikas. The Catholic bishops called on their flock to vote for "Anschluss" and Tyroleans registered 98.9 per cent "Yes".

They felt rewarded by the almost-immediate economic improvement, including a spectacular rise in the tourist trade, and were greatly impressed by the efficiency of the Nazi Party, the Hitler Youth movement and the Reich Labour Service. The first feelings of disquiet came with Nazi attacks on the Catholic church. Anti-semitism remained a marginal phenomenon in the Tyrol, if only because historical resistance to the Toleranzpatent had encouraged very few Jews to settle there. Meagre anti-Nazi resistance came from the few local Marxists and Catholic conservatives disillusioned by Hitler's leaving South Tyrol in the hands of Mussolini.

Because of its geographical isolation, Tyrol had a relatively quiet time in World War II—until the 1943 Allied air raids on armaments factories and traffic junctions at Innsbruck, Hall and Wörgl. American troops marched into Innsbruck on May 3, 1945. American occupation troops proved popular, but some Tyroleans feared that the French who followed might harbour resentments in light of local hostility to Napoleon in 1809. But the French had more immediate preoccupations in Indochina and cut their occupying force to a bare minimum until their departure in 1955.

With the conservative Volkspartei once again dominating regional politics, the Tyrol has since gone its own quiet way. The province prospers as a haven for winter sportsmen and summer tourists. Today, as so often in its history, the most important people in Tyrol are inn-keepers.

Plaits, hats, cowbells and tubas: Tyrol holds on to its old customs.

Where to Go

Compact as the Tyrol may be, it is not easy to cover the whole area during one stay—even if you have three or four weeks' holiday at your disposal. We therefore suggest you concentrate on one area, perhaps making an excursion or two into some of the others described in this section.

We've divided the province into four areas. In each of them you'll find a selection of resort towns from which to choose a base for tours of the surrounding countryside. Obviously the most convenient way to do this, if you can, is by car. But Austria offers a delightful and remarkably efficient alternative: the postal bus *(Postautobus)*. The bright yellow conveyances run by the national post office carry mail—and passengers—to outlying villages. It's easy to organize excursions and hikes according to the excellent timetables avail-

able from the Post Office Traffic Office *(Postverkehrsbüro)* in the major town of your chosen area.

Whether you base yourself in the western Tyrol (the Lechtal and Upper Inn Valley), in the northern section around Kitzbühel and the Kaisergebirge, or in East Tyrol near Lienz, you should also try to make a trip—a smooth journey by *Autobahn*—to the capital of Innsbruck and its environs for a more complete sense of Tyrol's history and traditions.

We also include a couple of excursions outside Austrian territory to Merano and Bolzano in South Tyrol, for a fascinating view of old Austrian culture with a new Italian accent, and to Salzburg, which lies so tantalizingly close to Kitzbühel and Kufstein.

The Zillertal offers a sunny contrast between alpine meadows and the rugged mountains.

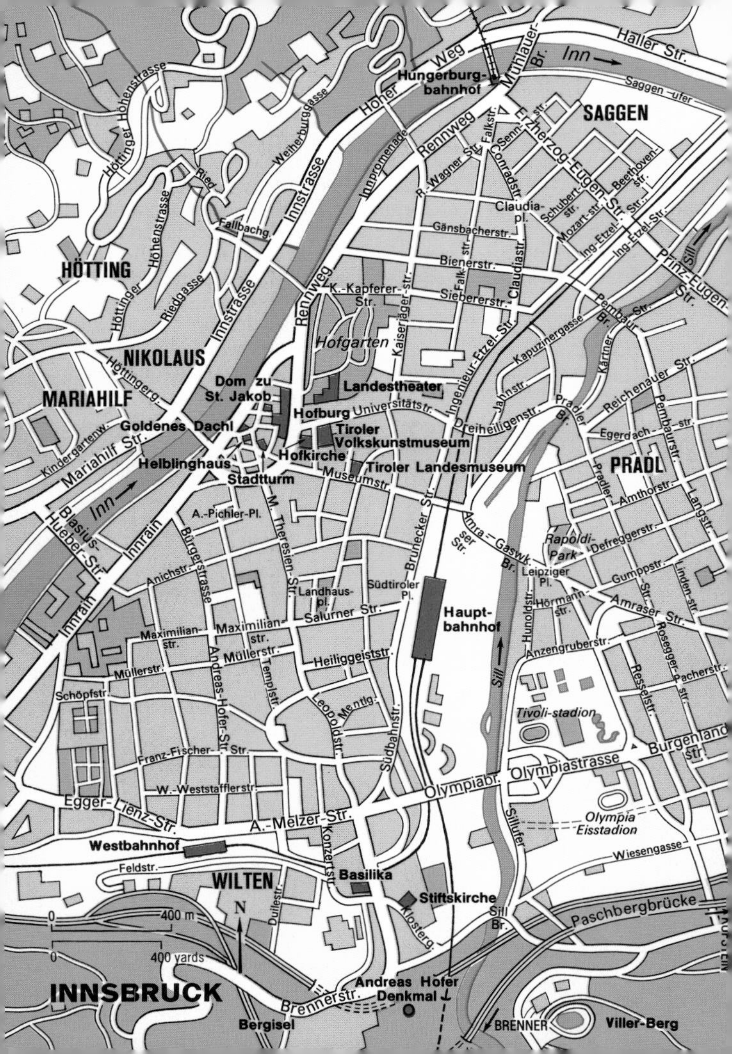

INNSBRUCK
HÖTTING
NIKOLAUS
MARIAHILF
SAGGEN
PRADL
WILTEN
Inn
Sill
Haller Str.
Mühlauer Br.
Saggen-ufer
Höher Weg
Hungerburg-bahnhof
Weiherburggasse
Innstrasse
Innpromenade
Rennweg
Höttinger Höhenstrasse
Höhenstrasse
Ried
Fallbachg.
Riedgasse
Höttinger
Höttingerg.
Erzherzog-Eugen-Str.
Falkstr.
Senn-str.
Conradstr.
R.-Wagner Str.
Claudia-pl.
Schubert-str.
Beethoven-str.
Mozart-str.
Ing.-Etzel-Str.
Gänsbacherstr.
Bienerstr.
Falk-str.
Claudiastr.
Siebererstr.
K.-Kapferer-Str.
Kaiserjäger-str.
Prinz-Eugen-Str.
Pembaur-Str.
Kapuzinergasse
Ingenieur-Etzel-Str.
Hofgarten
Landestheater
Dom zu St. Jakob
Hofburg
Universitätsstr.
Tiroler Volkskunstmuseum
Goldenes Dachl
Hofkirche
Helblinghaus
Stadtturm
Tiroler Landesmuseum
Kindergartenw.
Mariahilf Str.
Museumstr.
Dreiheiligenstr.
Jahnstr.
Pradler Br.
Kärtner Str.
Reichenauer Str.
Egerdach-str.
Pembaurstr.
Pradler Str.
Amthorstr.
Langstr.
Blasius-Hueber-Str.
Innrain
A.-Pichler-Pl.
M. Theresien-Str.
Bürgerstrasse
Brunecker Str.
Amraser Str.
Gaswk. Br.
Rapoldi-Park
Defreggerstr.
Leipziger Pl.
Gumppstr.
Linden-str.
Anichstr.
Landhaus-pl.
Südtiroler Pl.
Hauptbahnhof
Hörmann-str.
Hunoldstr.
Salurner Str.
Maximilian-str.
Müllerstr.
Heiliggeiststr.
Anzengruberstr.
Andreas-Hofer-Str.
Templstr.
Rosegger-str.
Resselstr.
Pacherstr.
Schöpfstr.
Leopoldstr.
Mentlg.
Tivoli-stadion
Südbahnstr.
Franz-Fischer-Str.
Burgenland str.
W.-Weststafflerstr.
Olympiabr.
Olympiastrasse
Egger-Lienz-Str.
A.-Melzer-Str.
Konzertstr.
Sillufer
Olympia Eisstadion
Westbahnhof
Wiesengasse
Feldstr.
Basilika
Stiftskirche
Duilestr.
Klosterg.
Sill Br.
Paschbergbrücke
0
400 m
400 yards
N
Brennerstr.
Andreas Hofer Denkmal
Bergisel
BRENNER
Viller-Berg

Central Tyrol

This region encompasses the capital of Innsbruck and surroundings: the larch and pine forests and flower-strewn meadows of the Stubaital, the 16th-century boom town of Schwaz, romantic Achensee and that warm and hospitable valley, the Zillertal.

Innsbruck

As the historic capital of the Tyrol since 1420, Innsbruck embraces the region's proudest traditions. The town nestles in the valley of the River Inn with the Karwendel mountains to the north and the domed Patscherkofel immediately to the south. The setting is dramatic, but when you first view the town flying into the local airport or driving along the *Autobahn,* you may feel that encroaching skyscrapers have not been kind to Innsbruck's silhouette. Just suspend judgement till you're in the old centre of the city, where the authentic charm and quiet majesty of the place still have the power to captivate.

Maria-Theresien-Strasse

Stand on the broadest part of the elegant Maria-Theresien-Strasse—which opens into a market square—and you'll see to the north the positively magic **panorama** of the old town's 15th- and 16th-century houses, town hall tower and cathedral domes set against the deep green fir and pine forest of the Karwendel foothills and the snowy peaks beyond.

This broad thoroughfare, now the town's main shopping street, was built in the 13th century as traffic over the Brenner Pass increased. It was later named after Empress Maria Theresa, who erected the **Triumphpforte** (Triumphal Arch) at the southern end in 1765 to celebrate the wedding of her son, the future Emperor Leopold II. The frieze on the north entablature depicts the untimely death of the empress's husband, Franz, which put an end to the wedding festivities. More truly triumphant, the **Annasäule** (St. Anne's Column) in the middle of the old marketplace celebrates a famous Tyrolean victory over the Bavarians on St. Anne's Day (July 26) in 1703.

Shining buildings of Tyrol's Renaissance and Baroque prosperity line Maria-Theresien-Strasse. On the east side of the street you can't miss the almost gaudy, mustard-coloured façade of the **Palais Fugger** (No. 45), town house of Count Hans Otto Fugger, one of the

chief financiers of the silver and copper mines at Schwaz. Like many of the Baroque edifices on the street, the house was built by a member of the Gumpp family of architects, in this case Johann Martin. He also designed the graceful façade which unites two buildings across the way into the **Palais Trapp** (No. 38). Take a look at the lovely gardens of this home of the Austrian-American Society and Italian Cultural Institute.

Right opposite is the grand **Altes Landhaus,** built by son Georg Anton Gumpp, which once sheltered the provincial government.

Innsbruck cherishes the Baroque façades of its venerable Altstadt.

Altstadt (Old Town)

Maria-Theresien-Strasse leads to **Herzog-Friedrich-Strasse,** which penetrates the very heart of old Innsbruck, the Altstadt. Now a pedestrian zone, it is bounded by the River Inn on the north-west; Marktgraben and Burggraben on the south trace what was once the town's semi-circular medieval protective moat. The massive, rampart-like outer walls of the buildings enclosing this historic precinct are known as *Erdbebenmauer* (earthquake walls); they were built after a tremor caused great destruction in 1670.

For all the modern accoutrements of souvenir shops and cafés, you enter an older, more sedate world as you stroll past Herzog-Friedrich-Strasse's arcaded 15th- and 16th-century houses, many of them ornamented with colourful Baroque façades.

Notice that the fast-food outlet lodged on the right-hand side in the old **Kohleggerhaus** (No. 35) respectfully preserves the arcade's 15th-century frescoes. On the left is the 16th-century **Trautsonhaus** (No. 22) with gabled bay windows and a nicely sculpted archway. Home of Tyrol's military leader Marshal Hans von Trautson, the late Gothic structure has graceful Renaissance details. The **Katzunghaus** (No. 16), now a pastry shop *(Konditorei),* has some fine 18th-century reliefs on its gables, portraying musicians, dancers and jousting knights.

Directly opposite is the **tower** *(Stadtturm)* of the old town hall *(Altes Rathaus)*. This solid structure, some 185 feet (57 m.) high was started in the 14th century but not completed till 1560. A stairway takes you up to a splendid **view** of the town and the surrounding mountains from eight different windows above the clock. The former caretaker's quarters lie under the green onion dome and belfry.

Back at street level, visit the **Alte Hofapotheke** next door, the venerable court apothecary; fine mahogany shelves hold porcelain jars containing mysterious potions—and bath salts.

The most decorative of the residences, **Helblinghaus,** stands at the corner of Herzog-Friedrich-Strasse as it turns west. Pink, turquoise and ivory stucco cherubim, acanthus wreaths and merry masks ornament the dazzling Rococo façade. Appropriately, this delightful piece of conspicuous consumption was once the home of Johannes Fischer, treasurer of the mint at nearby Hall.

The house provides a fitting frame for Innsbruck's grand-

Good coffee and violin music remind you you're in Austria.

est monument, the **Goldenes Dachl,** a loggia built onto what was then Emperor Maximilian I's Innsbruck residence *(Neuer Hof).* Literally "little golden roof", the loggia—a royal box from which to view tournaments—is the very symbol of the emperor's special attachment to Innsbruck. It was commissioned at the end of the 15th century to celebrate Maximilian's marriage, his second, to Bianca Maria Sforza, daughter of the Duke of Milan.

In addition to the brilliance of some 2,700 gilded copper shingles on the roof, the loggia is notable for the relief panels on the second-storey box, sculpted by Nikolaus Türing. Of the two central panels, the left shows Maximilian with both his wives; the new one holds a golden apple for the tournament champion and the prettier first wife, Mary of Burgundy, looks a little wistful in her French double-coned headdress. The right-hand panel portrays the court fool and the royal counsellor (flanking the Emperor), traditionally symbols of good and bad advice—without any indication of who gave which. The outer panels show some very acrobatic Moorish dancers. At the first-floor level are coats-of-arms of territories which Maximilian

possessed or merely dreamed of possessing. Although the original reliefs are kept in the Landesmuseum (see p. 39), their colours have faded. The polychrome copies here give a better idea of how the loggia looked in its heyday.

Just east of the Goldenes Dachl, the narrow Pfarrgasse leads to the cathedral, **Dom zu St. Jakob,** which stands in a tranquil square shaded by maples and copper beeches and surrounded by some of the town's oldest surviving houses. Note in particular No. 3, Mösleinhaus, dating back to the 13th century. The cathedral was built in 1722 to replace a Gothic edifice devastated by earthquake; it served as parish church until Innsbruck took over the diocese from Bressanone (Brixen) when South Tyrol was ceded to Italy.

Designed by Johann Jakob Herkommer, the late Baroque exterior, is a masterpiece of restraint in an age not known for architectural austerity: of massive hewn stone, it is graced with two very solid onion-dome towers on the west front and a broad, but still modest, dome over the choir. More conventionally exuberant is the interior, executed by the Asam brothers of Münich. Cosmas painted the ceiling with *trompe l'oeil* frescoes and Egid Quirin modelled the intricate stucco work. There's a richly sculpted pulpit by Nikolaus Moll, but the cathedral's most prized artwork is the Lucas Cranach *Mariahilf* (Madonna with Child) over the high altar, a painting copied on countless house façades throughout the Tyrol.

Come back down Pfarrgasse and turn east on Hofgasse, site of the 16th-century **Deutschordenshaus,** built for the German Order of Knights, notable for its ornamental façade and fine, wrought-iron sign for the glazier's trade. But the main attraction lies across the street at No. 12: the 15th-century **Burgriesenhaus,** home of Nikolaus Haidl, Archduke Sigmund's court giant (everybody should have one), the husband of Sigmund's illegitimate daughter. Haidl's statue, with cudgel, today guards a night club. Notice the unusually high entrance.

An integral part of the old town is its bridge, the **Alte Innbrücke,** on the north-west side. This gives a delightful view of one of Innsbruck's pleasantest aspects, the swift-flowing River Inn, silver in spring, green in high summer.

Hofburg and Hofkirche

Facing away from the old town, the bright yellow and white **Hofburg** at the north end of Burggraben is Maria Theresa's Baroque unification of the once sprawling Gothic ducal residence, completed long after the Habsburg dukes had deserted the Tyrol for Vienna. The opulent Rococo decoration and furnishings, particularly in the **Riesensaal** (Giant's Hall), reflect Maria Theresa's imperial glories. The best view of the palace is from the elaborate **Leopolds-**

brunnen, a fountain erected for Archduke Leopold V, whose equestrian statue is spurred on by Diana and sundry nymphs, while a lovely Leda is preoccupied with her swan.

Have a rest in the palace gardens, **Hofgarten,** now a pleasant little park given over to chess players and pigeons, with chestnut trees, sycamores and weeping willows.

South of the palace stands the **Hofkirche** (court church), unprepossessing from the outside but nonetheless a "must" for the magnificent, monumental **tomb** of Maximilian—minus his remains (see p. 18). With this incredible piece of self-glorification, Maximilian wanted to prove he was justified in calling himself the Holy Roman Emperor: *holy* by reason of the Habsburg's patron saints—23 of 100 planned statues adorn the Hofkirche's rear gallery; *Roman* by dint of the Caesars of whom he claimed to be the legitimate successor—21 of a planned 34 busts of Roman emperors line the north gallery; and *emperor* as a descendant of Clovis, King of the Franks and Theoderic, King of the Ostrogoths—even

The Hofburg is dwarfed by the majestic Karwendel mountains.

King Arthur of England and the Round Table. Of the planned 40 larger-than-life-size statues, 28 now-blackened bronzes stand perpetual watch over the wrought-iron cage protecting Maximilian's white marble cenotaph.

Among the army of artists recruited for this gigantic task was Albrecht Dürer, who designed Theoderic (fifth on the right as you go towards the altar) and Arthur (eighth on the right). The sculptors relied for authenticity on contemporary portraits; because none existed for Ferdinand of Portugal (seventh on the right), he is shown with a visor covering his face.

Left of the entrance, in a corner all to itself, is the tomb of Tyrolean resistance hero Andreas Hofer, his statue draped with a black flag which mourns the loss of his native South Tyrol to Italy.

Archduke Ferdinand II and his commoner-wife Philippine Welser lie buried in the splendid **Silberne Kapelle,** which takes its name from the silver Madonna on the altar.

Museums

Next door to the Hofkirche in Universitätsstrasse, the **Tiroler Volkskunstmuseum** (Museum of Popular Arts) offers wonderfully rich—and often very moving—insights into the everyday life of old Tyrol. Many towns in the region have a museum of local lore *(Heimatmuseum),* but this one, housed in an old Franciscan monastery, is truly outstanding. Displayed in the cloisters are ornate wooden sleighs with monster figureheads. When not gliding through the snow, many Tyroleans obviously spent long winter nights constructing elaborate manger scenes (exhibited on the ground floor); a host of angels, shepherds, kings and saints accompany the Holy Family. The models in polychrome wood or delicate porcelain show how this ancient hobby formed part of the region's intense religious life.

Upstairs are the reconstituted interiors of centuries-old farmhouses with authentic wooden furnishings and wall panelling, coffered ceilings, copper utensils, massive glazed-tile stoves (which served as very cosy bedsteads in winter) and intricate wrought-iron door and window fixtures. Look out for the bizarre towel-rack held up by a bust that is half-skeleton (a serpent lurks in the rib cage) and half-woman (an understandably worried-looking lady). The exhibition of peasant costumes includes that of a splendidly wild vineyard warden *(Wein-*

berghüter) from South Tyrol, armed with a pike and gigantic headdress profusely decorated with the feathers and fur of all the game he was wont to hunt.

Innsbruck's fine arts collection is housed in the **Tiroler Landesmuseum** or Ferdinandeum (Museumstrasse 15). In addition to the original reliefs from the Goldenes Dachl, the museum has some exquisite Romanesque and Gothic sculptures salvaged from churches redecorated in the Baroque style. The most important works by Tyrolean artists include Michael Pacher's 15th-century portrait of St. Catherine and Andreas Haller's early 16th-century **Flagellants' Altar** (complete with the original whips and chains). A small Dutch and Flemish collection boasts an early Rembrandt portrait of his father, a Jan van Goyen landscape and a fine Quentin Metsys *Madonna and Child.*

Wilten and Bergisel

On the southern outskirts of Innsbruck, Wilten, site of the ancient Roman camp of Veldidena, possesses two noteworthy churches. The 17th-century **Stiftskirche St. Laurentius** is a work of the Gumpp family, Christoph, Johann Martin and Georg Anton. Complementing an attractively warm ochre-and-red exterior are the rich black-and-gold altars inside, beneath a white stucco, vaulted ceiling. Across Leopoldstrasse stands **Basilika Wilten,** the triumphant jewel of Tyrolean Rococo—gleaming yellow without, a blaze of colour within. Note Matthäus Günther's frescoes of *Esther* and *Judith,* a forceful celebration of this supremely feminine style.

History buffs might like to make the 15-minute climb (or faster drive) to the Andreas Hofer monument on **Bergisel** battlefield at the southern end of Leopoldstrasse. Here the Tyrolean militia heroically conquered Napoleon's Bavarian allies in 1809. Also the site of the 1964 and 1976 Olympic ski jump, the 2,460-foot- (750-m.) high plateau affords a fine **view** of the city and the Karwendel mountains beyond.

Schloss Ambras

Solid-enough fortress in the Middle Ages, Ambras (southeast of town off Amraser Strasse) was turned into a palace *(Lustschloss)* by Ferdinand II for his wife Philippine in the 16th century. This charming little pile overlooks the Inn valley. One of the highlights of a visit is the beautiful **armoury** collection. Look out

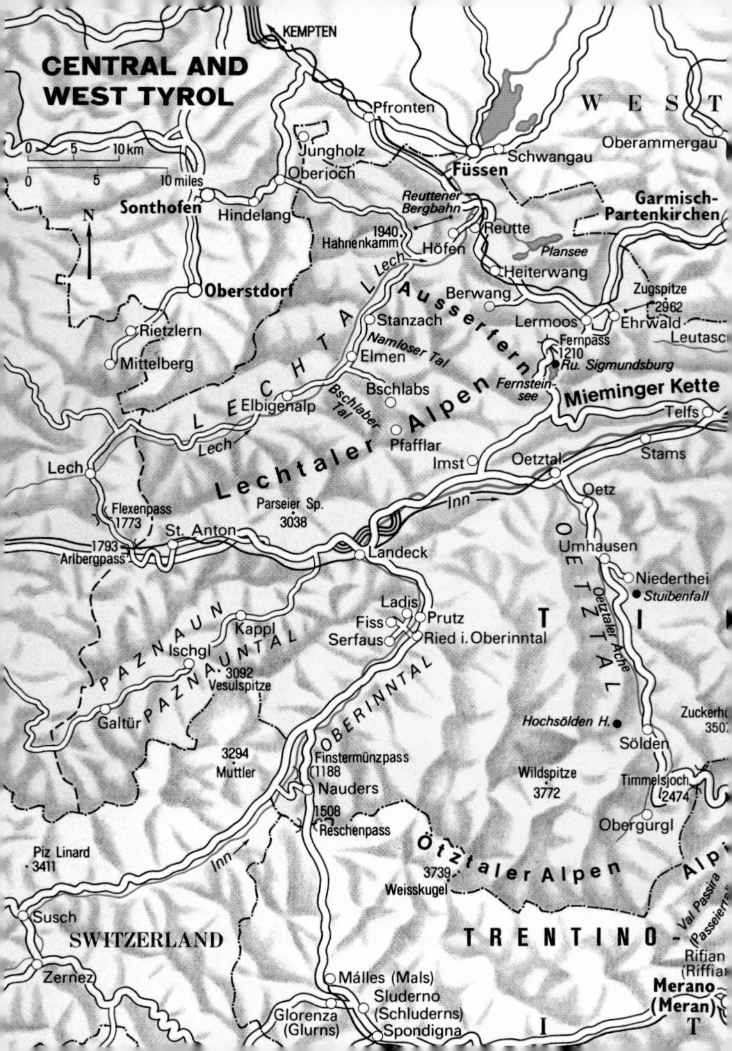
CENTRAL AND WEST TYROL
0 5 10 km
0 5 10 miles
N
KEMPTEN
Pfronten
Jungholz
Oberjoch
Füssen
Schwangau
Oberammergau
WEST
Garmisch-Partenkirchen
Sonthofen
Hindelang
Reuttener Bergbahn
Reutte
1940
Hahnenkamm
Höfen
Plansee
Heiterwang
Oberstdorf
Berwang
Zugspitze
2962
Lermoos
Ehrwald
Leutasch
Rietzlern
Stanzach
Fernpass
1210
Mittelberg
Elmen
Namloser Tal
Ru. Sigmundsburg
Ausserfern
Fernstein-see
Mieminger Kette
LECHTAL
Lech
Bschlabs
Elbigenalp
Bschlaber Tal
Telfs
Pfafflar
Lechtaler Alpen
Imst
Oetztal
Stams
Lech
Oetz
Parseier Sp.
3038
Flexenpass
1773
Inn
St. Anton
1793
Arlbergpass
Landeck
Umhausen
Niederthei
Stuibenfall
Ladis
Fiss
Prutz
Serfaus
Ried i. Oberinntal
Kappl
PAZNAUN
Ischgl
PAZNAUNTAL
3092
Vesulspitze
OETZTAL
Oetztaler Ache
Galtür
OBERINNTAL
Hochsölden H.
Sölden
3294
Muttler
Finstermünzpass
1188
Nauders
1508
Reschenpass
Wildspitze
3772
Timmelsjoch
2474
Obergurgl
Piz Linard
3411
Inn
Ötztaler Alpen
3739
Weisskugel
Susch
SWITZERLAND
TRENTINO
Val Passira (Passeiertal)
Rifian (Riffian)
Zernez
Málles (Mals)
Sluderno (Schluderns)
Glorenza (Glurns)
Spondigna
Merano (Meran)

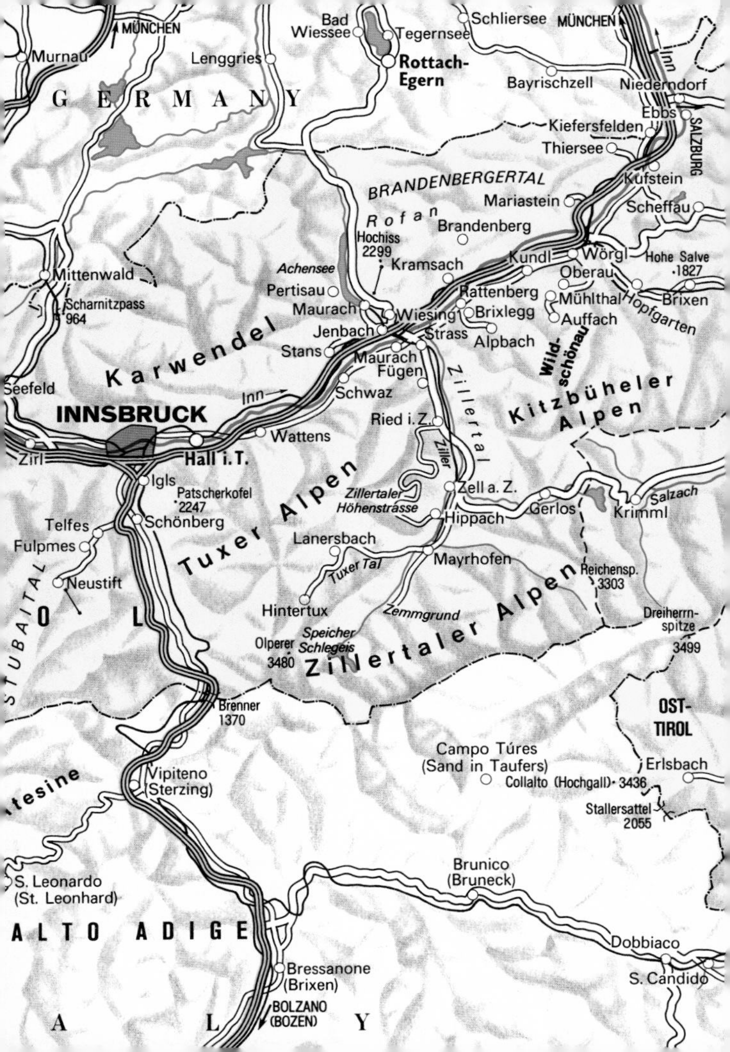

MÜNCHEN
Murnau
Lenggries
Bad Wiessee
Tegernsee
Rottach-Egern
Schliersee
MÜNCHEN
Bayrischzell
Niederndorf
Inn
GERMANY
Ebbs
Kiefersfelden
SALZBURG
Thiersee
Kufstein
BRANDENBERGERTAL
Mariastein
Scheffau
Rofan
Brandenberg
Hochiss 2299
Kundl
Wörgl
Hohe Salve 1827
Achensee
Kramsach
Oberau
Mittenwald
Pertisau
Rattenberg
Mühlthal
Brixen
Scharnitzpass 964
Maurach
Wiesing
Brixlegg
Auffach
Hopfgarten
Jenbach
Strass
Alpbach
Karwendel
Stans
Maurach
Wildschönau
Fügen
Seefeld
Schwaz
Zillertal
Kitzbüheler Alpen
Inn
INNSBRUCK
Ried i. Z.
Wattens
Zirl
Hall i. T.
Ziller
Igls
Tuxer Alpen
Patscherkofel 2247
Zillertaler Höhenstrasse
Zell a. Z.
Salzach
Gerlos
Krimml
Telfes
Schönberg
Hippach
Fulpmes
Lanersbach
Mayrhofen
Tuxer Tal
Reichensp. 3303
Neustift
STUBAITAL
Hintertux
Zemmgrund
Zillertaler Alpen
Dreiherrnspitze 3499
O
L
Speicher Schlegeis
Olperer 3480
Brenner 1370
OST-TIROL
Campo Túres (Sand in Taufers)
Erlsbach
Vipiteno (Sterzing)
Collalto (Hochgall) 3436
atesine
Stallersattel 2055
Brunico (Bruneck)
S. Leonardo (St. Leonhard)
ALTO ADIGE
Dobbiaco
S. Candido
Bressanone (Brixen)
BOLZANO (BOZEN)
A
L
Y

for the cute little suits of armour worn on festive occasions by five- and six-year-old royal tykes. A great curiosity is the **Kunst- und Wunderkammer** (Chamber of Art and Wonders), which dates from a time when Renaissance princes delighted in collecting weird and grotesque objects, paintings and sculptures. Don't miss the portrait of gruesome Gregor Baci, a 16th-century dwarf who went about with a lance through his head.

Stepping out on market day is an earnest business for the children.

Stubaital

A one-hour's drive south from Innsbruck provides the perfect initiation into the beauties of the Tyrol's alpine valleys. From the Schönberg exit of the Brenner *Autobahn* (A13), the Stubai valley rises gradually through forests of larch and pine, past brilliant green meadows up to summer skiing slopes.

First stop is **Fulpmes,** centre of Stubaital's blacksmith traditions, famous for the manufacture of mountain-climbing equipment. Down by the village stream, a few water-driven smithies still turn out Stubai ice-picks and pitons. The local Blacksmith's Museum *(Schmiedemuseum)* is worth a visit. Take a look, too, at the slim, elegant design of the parish church, **Pfarrkirche zum hl. Vitus,** one of three in the valley built in the 18th century by architect-priest Franz de Paula Penz (who also designed the Wilten basilica in Innsbruck). Before continuing up the valley, double back to **Telfes,** Penz's home parish. His little St. Pankraz Church, a veritable jewel, looks much bigger inside thanks to Josef Anton Zoller's airy fresco over the transept. The Telfes larch meadows make a great place to break in your walking shoes.

Neustift is the valley's principal resort, a bright and cheerful village with an unusually large parish church. **St. Georg** dominates the south-western end of the valley with its tall, bulb-domed bell tower. Penz's last work, the church was completed in 1774. From Neustift, take the cable car (Stubaier Gletscherbahn) up to year-round skiing and tobogganing on **Stubai Glacier,** 10,500 feet (3,200 m.) above sea level. Even if you're not in the mood for winter sports in the summer, the cable car trip is worth it just for the view.

Hall

Just 10 kilometres east of Innsbruck, Hall is a medieval town of considerable character, built on a hillside overlooking the River Inn. There are delightful narrow streets of old houses leaning at odd angles and a picturesque main square. Stroll back to the time when Hall, a centre of the salt-mining industry (its name is a Celtic word for salt), was twice the size of Innsbruck. Even after Innsbruck's elevation to capital of the Tyrol, Hall remained vitally important for its strategic position on the river—and as the place where the money was. The mint was moved from Merano to Hall in the 15th century.

Burg Hasegg, on the south side of the city walls, looms over a row of pretty, ochre-painted houses with vegetable gardens irrigated from a tributary of the Inn. This is the fortress that housed the old mint, closed in 1809; the tower *(Münzerturm)* still stands as a proud symbol of past glories. Inside the fortress, visit the mint museum *(Alte Münze),* where you can see and even try your hand at the minting of coins and medals on sturdy black-steel machinery. The mint was briefly returned to active duty at the time of the 1976 Winter Olympics, when it issued commemorative 100-Schilling coins. A mining museum *(Bergbaumuseum)* shows you how they used to dig out the salt of the earth, all-important for preserving food in the days before refrigeration.

Make your way up to the **Oberer Stadtplatz** (Upper Town Square), graced with pleasant fountains watched over by a crowned Madonna. On the south side, **St. Nikolaus,** the parish church, is a Gothic edifice whose renovation in the 18th century set the high altar at an intriguing, oblique angle to the nave. In the choir, there is a fine late Gothic (1420) sculpture of Jesus on a donkey, a traditional feature of Palm Sunday processions. In the

small, two-storeyed **Magdalenen-Kapelle** a notable 15th-century *Day of Judgement* fresco spans the south wall of the upper chapel. The most attractive façade on the Oberer Stadtplatz—and one appropriate to Hall's grand civic past—is that of the Gothic **Rathaus** (Town Hall). Gaily decorated on the battlement walls with coats-of-arms, it also boasts a splendidly carved, wooden-beamed council chamber—the Ratssaal.

Schwaz

Economically once one of the most important towns in the German empire—with 30,000 inhabitants in the 16th century, it was second in size in Austria only to Vienna—Schwaz has suffered more than most Tyrolean towns from the ravages of war. Napoleon's armies in 1809 and Allied bombardments

Dirndl and jeans coexist happily. Tratzberg's frescoed courtyard.

in World War II left few vestiges of "Silver Schwaz, Mother of all Mining", as it used to be known. Copper was mined long before the Roman conquest, and silver was discovered in time to finance Habsburg ambitions during the Middle Ages.

The one street to give an idea of the 16th-century townscape is Franz-Joseph-Strasse, which curves gently round to the striking façade of the **Pfarrkirche Unserer Lieben Frau** (Parish Church of the Madonna). The stepped-gabled west front was inspired by Munich's Gothic town hall, while Rattenberg's church of St. Virgil provided an appropriate civic solution to a Schwaz social problem of the 1450s. The growth of the mining community was causing overflows at the church, and the merchant classes didn't enjoy rubbing shoulders with the grimy miners—who didn't like the snooty merchants, either. So it was decided to create two double-naved churches under one roof, each with its own choir, with the roof over the choirs split into two. Inside, the wooden wall separating the two congregations (miners to the right) has gone, leaving the interior a spacious and harmonious whole, adorned with a beautiful Gothic stone **baptismal font** with Renaissance wooden cover. At the entrance to the miner's choir *(Knappenchor),* look for the **Anna-Altar,** three Gothic statues of Saints Anne, Elisabeth and Ursula subsequently placed in an elaborate Baroque setting. On the side altar leading to the burghers' choir *(Bürgerchor)* is a lovely Gothic Madonna from 1430. The gravestones in the Knappenchor reveal that two members of the great Fugger dynasty, which helped finance the mines, chose to be buried with the workers.

On the south side of town, the **Franziskanerkloster** (Franciscan Monastery) preserves in its cloisters—against severe attacks of humidity—some fine, early 16th-century frescoes. These scenes of Jesus's Passion and Apotheosis were created by Wilhelm von Schwaben. They are close in style to coloured woodcuts, and the colour in the detailed portrayals is subdued. The angels, coats-of-arms and floral motifs on the ceilings were added in 1600. East of the monastery, a road leads to **Burg Freundsberg,** fortress home of the military family that dominated Schwaz in the 12th century. It now houses an interesting museum of local lore *(Heimatmuseum),* displaying mining equipment and furnishings from miners' homes.

Schloss Tratzberg (a few kilometres north-east of Schwaz) has been turned over the centuries from a formidable medieval stronghold defending the heights above the River Inn into a charming palace for the magnates of the silver mines, first the Tänzls, then the Fuggers. The opulent Renaissance interiors have been lovingly restored by the present tenants, the family of Count Enzenberg. The elaborate, wood-panelled coffered ceilings, richly carved doors and cabinets and, above all, the warm tones of the amber-and-white arcaded inner courtyard contrast strikingly with the explicitly forbidding exterior, conceived to discourage intruders. Today, summer visitors are welcome. An extensive pictorial family tree covers the walls of the **Habsburgersaal**, portraying 148 kinsmen of Emperor Maximilian (who sold the castle to the Tänzls for a song). On the same first floor, the Fuggerkammer and Fuggerstube are furnished in the grand style to which the great merchants were accustomed. In the ground-floor Rüstkammer there's an interesting collection of old armour.

Achensee

Achensee, 5½ miles (9 km.) long and over half a mile (1 km.) wide, is the Tyrol's largest lake. This beautiful expanse of clear blue water cuts like a Norwegian fjord through the valley separating the Karwendel mountains to the west and the Rofangebirge to the east.

Half the pleasure of the lake is getting there. You have two charming alternatives. The **Achenseebahn,** oldest steam rack or cog railway in Europe, climbs some 1,440 feet (440 m.) along a route of about 7 kilometres from JENBACH to the lake terminus at SEESPITZ. The 40-minute ride takes you up through shady mountain forests with sudden clearings that afford wonderful views over the Inn valley and the beginning

High Life on the Lake

The Renaissance-era Archduke Ferdinand II built a whole fleet of pleasure boats for his Achensee hunting parties. He had racing skiffs, a ship for fishing, a ship for shooting, one for cooking wild duck and fish, another for storing wine. And, housing the state room where he held his water-borne banquets, was a richly ornamented Venetian galley propelled by 15 oarsmen dressed all in emerald green.

of the Zillertal. If you're driving, the broad motorway of the Kanzelkehre winds up through the mountains and along the lake's eastern shore with similar lovely **panoramas** on the 25 kilometres from STRASS via WIESING.

The resort towns of **Maurach** at the southern end and

Despite the altitude, Achensee's water is warm enough for a swim.

Pertisau on the west shore provide first-class facilities for fishing the lake's rainbow trout, perch, pike and roach, and for the whole panoply of water sports. If the waters are

clear and tranquil it's in small part thanks to the ban on private motor boats. But you can take a romantic steamboat cruise, enhanced by sweet music and the soft light flooding the Geissalm cliffs north of Pertisau. From its terminus at the southern end of the lake, the Rofanseilbahn (cable car) whisks up to the Erfurter Hütte, 6,033 feet (1,834 m.) above sea level, starting point for exhilarating walks through the **Rofan's** alpine meadows and craggy landscape.

Zillertal

Broad, bright green, bordered but not hemmed in by the Tuxer Alps to the west and the Kitzbühel Alps to the east, the Zillertal boasts a mild, sunny climate and a correspondingly warm and hospitable population. Geologically the classical example of the U-shaped glacier formation, the Zillertal seems to many the most cheerful valley in the Tyrol.

In a total of ten hours, hikers can walk its length from Strass, at the junction of the Inn and Ziller rivers to Mayrhofen, at the foot of the Zillertal Alps, near the border with Italy. The 30-kilometre road along the river takes scarcely more than half-an-hour's actual driving time. If you're not planning to stay there—its resort towns do make excellent bases for further explorations—make your way to the southern end of the valley and start your visit there. Without a car or good hiking legs, you can still take the delightful little **Zillertalbahn,** a steam train which makes frequent stops on the trip between

Jenbach and Mayrhofen. On Fridays and Saturdays they let passengers play engine driver.

Mayrhofen, blessed with an annual average of 249 sunny days (there are only eight days when winds reach storm force), is the smiling queen of Zillertal resort towns. Though it has no particular cultural monuments to boast of, the village can be justly proud of its characterful architecture: the older, dark-timbered houses with splendidly carved balconies running all around the upper storeys, decorated with a profusion of seasonal flowers.

Set in the "orchestra stalls" of a theatre that has the Zillertal Alps as its backdrop, Mayrhofen cannily manages to offer modern, efficient hotel and sports facilities, stylish shops and nightclubs, while not losing contact with the valley's traditions, its cuisine and colourful costume. Without giving the impression of "putting it on for the tourists", the people walk around in time-honoured *Tracht* dresses or loden jackets and leather breeches.

The town is the perfect springboard for excursions, on foot or by car, into the four tributary valleys (the "Gründe") penetrating the southern mountains—dramatic countryside of narrow, densely wooded gorges among sheer cliffs, with huge rocks dislodged ages ago by earthquakes onto the valley floor. There's summer skiing on the Hintertux glacier, at the south-west end of the Tuxertal. Heart-stopping kayak races are held in the rushing, rock-strewn waters of the Zemmgrund. The valley road leads (via a toll booth) to the spectacular mountain reservoir of the **Speicher Schlegeis.** Take a walk along the reassuringly wide parapet of the dam wall. You'll be looking down at 4,510,364,000 cubic feet (127,700,000 cubic m.) of water.

Five kilometres north of Mayrhofen, in the pretty village of HIPPACH, is the road that leads to the **Zillertaler Höhenstrasse,** a toll road, which follows the crest of the valley's western mountain ridge. The toll road takes you up, up and away from the crowds for a walking tour among fields of alpine violets and roses, lady's slipper and, of course, edelweiss.

You can ride along this pleasant mountain road all the way to RIED, but an earlier exit leads down to **Zell am Ziller,** the valley's chief town and very pleasant resort, some-

Zell am Ziller's green steeples were once in Salzburg's diocese.

what calmer than Mayrhofen. Visit 18th-century **Pfarrkirche St. Veit,** on the "Salzburg side" of the valley and still part of the Salzburg diocese. So the spire of the church is green rather than Tyrolean red. An admirable ceiling fresco by Franz Anton Zeiller covers the nave with a vast portrayal of the Holy Trinity.

Some 8 kilometres from the northern mouth of the Zillertal, **Fügen** is perhaps the most picturesque of the valley's resort towns, nestling as it does against the sheltering slope of the Fügenberg among larch and pine forests and sunny meadows. An easy walk takes you up the mountainside to the lovely little 15th-century church of **St. Pankraz,** scarcely more than a chapel but much favoured for romantic weddings (are there other kinds?); the town hires out a horse-drawn coach—or sleigh in winter—to take the "Just Marrieds" off to their honeymoon. Fügen's parish church is the late Gothic **Mariä Himmelfahrt** (Assumption). Its modern altar stands in front of impressive polychrome sculptures of the 12 apostles from 1495. The side altars have touchingly simple Gothic statues of the *Madonna and Child* (left) and the *Mourning of Christ* (right).

West Tyrol

Tranquil West Tyrol takes in the Lechtal—the valley that sweeps south-west of Reutte—and the Oberinntal or Upper Inn Valley, where stands historic Stams Abbey. Here, too, are the smart skiing meccas of Seefeld and St. Anton, and the Oetztal, site of Tyrol's highest waterfall, the Stuibenfall.

Lechtal

Life in the region known as Ausserfern—beyond the Fern Pass, which leads over the Lechtaler Alps into Germany—is quieter, more secluded, more relaxed, perhaps, than in the busier resorts around Innsbruck. The Ausserfern's centre is **Reutte,** a friendly market town commanding the Lechtal. Reutte has no remarkable churches or imposing architecture, but its houses from the Baroque period are cosy enough, with their carved wooden beams and balconies, wrought-iron window grills and colourful façades. Many of the latter were painted in the 18th century by gifted members of the local Zeiller family. Their residence, the Zeillerhäuschen (Untergsteig 1), the Bürgermeisteramt (Mayor's Office), the Goldene Krone and Schwarzer Adler inns in Obermarkt are among the best examples. The **Heimatmuseum** displays an admirable collection of paintings by Franz Anton Zeiller, cousin Johann Jakob and father Paul.

But Reutte is, above all, a starting point for some delightful excursions into the surrounding mountains, lakes and forests. South-east of town are two lovely lakes, the **Heiterwanger See** and **Plansee.** Joined by a canal, they offer ample opportunities for sailing and trout fishing or a leisurely cruise—best at sunset—in a motor boat. A 10-minute ride on the mountain railway *(Reuttener Bergbahn)* or a bracing two-hour walk from the village of HÖFEN takes you up to the spectacular **Alpine Flower Garden** *(Alpenblumengarten)* on the Hahnenkamm (Reutte's own version of the cock's-comb mountain silhouette that has made Kitzbühel so famous). In lovingly tended meadows, you can wander among cyclamen and purple paschal flowers, cowslips, lady's slipper and snowdrops. And how does *your* garden grow?

As you make your way south beside the River Lech, you'll be tempted to explore some of the little valleys where the landscape is distinctively decorated with battalions of hay stacks lined up in formation across the fields. East of STANZACH—where St. Michael's church has a fine altar painting by Johann Jakob Zeiller—the **Namloser Tal** meanders charmingly up to some lovely mountain picnic grounds on the Gufelalm. Running south-east from ELMEN is a valley with probably the nicest name in all Tyrol, the **Bschlaber Tal.** The village names whisper in your ears like the wind in the mountain elms, as you pass the village of BSCHLABS, with its exquisite onion-domed chapel perched on the hillside, and on up through the forests to PFAFFLAR. The panoramas of steep gorges and gushing waterfalls opposite gently sloping cornfields provide a matching poetry.

Elbigenalp, oldest parish in the Lechtal—and the delicately painted house façades make it one of the prettiest—is a good final destination for this excursion. The parish church, **St. Nikolaus,** is a Gothic edifice completely, but not unsuccessfully, reconstructed in Baroque style. Gothic vestiges include the slim choir, the tall windows of the tower and a stone baptismal font of 1411. The Zeiller family's grandiose frescoes are an awe-inspiringly triumphant celebration of Christianity. This is the very heart of the "Holy Land of Tyrol".

Oberinntal

(Upper Inn Valley)

If you're making your way west from Innsbruck, take the *Autobahn* exit for Garmisch-Partenkirchen to see what the famous skiing mecca of **Seefeld** looks like in summer. The Karwendel's alpine meadows are a glorious riot of colour—purple clover, yellow columbine, blue cornflowers and a panoply of wild roses and daisies that leave the snow a distant and not-at-all regretted memory. If you like to combine luxury accommodation and smart boutiques with a little sport and some robust mountain hikes, this is the place. Very little of the old town remains, but St. Oswald, the parish church, is worth a visit for its Gothic porch. A finely sculpted relief graces the archway.

You can while the time away fishing—or pay a visit to Stams.

The *Autobahn* west of Innsbruck ends in TELFS. From there you can travel on up the mountain road that winds through the Mieminger Kette (chain) to the superb vistas of the **Fernpass.** Just south of the pass, you'll see Sigmundsburg, the ruined hunting lodge of spendthrift Duke Sigmund, on an island in Fernsteinsee. The road continues down through dense larch and pine forests to the lively resorts of Lermoos and Ehrwald.

Lermoos has an attractive parish church, St. Katharina, notable for a light and airy Rococo interior, highlighted by a gleaming pulpit and finely carved sculptures of St. George and St. John. There are some nice old houses in the upper village *(Oberdorf)* south of the main road.

Ehrwald is popular with sportsmen. From here a cable car runs up the sunny side of the **Zugspitze,** at 9,716 feet (2,962 m.) the tallest mountain

in Germany—but Germany has the cold northern slope. Dress up warm, since the peak is always snow-covered, and enjoy the grand view with a heart-warming grog in the panoramic restaurant at the top. Hardy hikers make their own way up to the cable-car half-way station. Hardier mountaineers climb all the way—"strenuous child's play", they call it.

Back down in the Inn valley, **Stift Stams** (Stams Abbey) is a summit of the Tyrol's monastic Baroque architecture. People are intrigued by the contrast between the splendour of the abbey church and monastery buildings and the Cistercian vows of poverty and asceticism. The Cistercians were invited to set up house here in 1273. The somewhat austere Romanesque basilica form chosen for the church dates from that time. But 18th century transformations completely altered the look of the abbey.

The interior pays almost overpowering homage to the glory of God and the divinely appointed rulers of Tyrol. On entering, you're confronted with the grandiose **Princes' Crypt** *(Fürstengruft),* above which stands a towering Crucifixion. Inspired by Maximilian's monumental tomb in Innsbruck (see pp. 37–38) are the gleaming polychrome-and-gilt statues of a dozen Tyrolean princes and princesses by Andreas Thamasch. The splendid high altar of gilded wood, carved by Bartholomäus Steinle in 1613, depicts the Tree of Life, a genealogy of Jesus, beginning with Adam and Eve. The whole is topped rather incongruously by a clock.

The church's imposing decoration also includes some magnificently carved choir stalls; Thamasch's lyrical *Madonna and Child* on the south wall, directly opposite the pulpit; and ornate wrought-iron gates, notably the Rosengitter at the Chapel of the Holy Blood *(Heilig-Blut-Kapelle).*

The juxtaposition of wealth and austerity is most apparent of all in **St. Bernard's Hall** *(Bernhardisaal),* built by the Gumpp family of Innsbruck in 1720. Sumptuous frescoes by Michael Hueber and Anton Zoller illustrate the ascetic life of Bernard of Clairvaux, founder of the Cistercian order. Subtle trompe l'oeil decoration and a purely ornamental upper gallery create a sense of opulent spaciousness in a room also known as the Princes' Hall *(Fürstensaal).* You might like to ponder the implications in the lovely cloister gardens.

Landeck has an attractive situation at the bend in the River Inn where, for south-bound travellers, the valley begins to narrow and climb along the old Roman road, Via Claudia Augusta, over the Reschen Pass in Italy. (Landeck also serves as a regional gateway to several west Tyrolean winter resorts with summer facilities you might like to investigate. **Ischgl,** in the Paznauntal, is one of the most popular targets. But the most celebrated is undoubtedly **St. Anton,** just a half-hour's drive from Landeck. The little shopping centre lies within a pedestrian zone west of the parish church, Mariahilf. This rather odd structure has one Baroque domed tower, built in 1691, and a very modern south tower of 1932.)

Back in the sunny Oberinntal, drive a dozen kilometres south to PRUTZ and park for an exhilarating and really very easy walk up to the delightful village of **Ladis** on the west side of the valley. (The lazy can drive back north from RIED.) You'll be rewarded with a look at some rare, 800-year-old houses; beautifully painted frescoes surround the bay windows. One in particular, Stockerhaus, illustrates stories from the Old and New Testaments, often with considerable humour. Nearby FISS also offers some fine gabled houses, and **Serfaus** provides the most modern resort facilities if you'd like to prolong your stay in this blessed little corner of the land.

At the southern end of the valley, guarded by the solid 14th-century **Schloss Naudersberg,** comes the dividing of the ways: one road forks off into Switzerland and another leads on to Italy.

Oetztal

This long valley—with steep, narrow gorges, dense, deep-green forests and a rushing torrent of a river abounding in craggy rocks—provides a stark contrast to the milder charms of the Zillertal (see p. 49). If the latter can be painted in primary colours, the Oetztal requires subtler, pastel shades. The landscape here is both less sentimental and more romantic—a good place to get away from the crowds.

And so the town of **Oetz** makes a more restrained, if nonetheless cheerful impression, characterized by the elegantly sober Gothic spire of its parish church, dedicated to Saints George and Nicholas. The tone is set by the noble allure of the **Gasthof zum Stern,** a venerable tavern with finely ornamented gabled windows over a Gothic arched doorway. On the opposite slope of the valley, you can bathe whatever aches you may suffer in the soothing, warm waters of the pretty **Piburger See.**

At UMHAUSEN a secondary road leads up to the **Stuibenfall,** Tyrol's highest waterfall. You'll get the best view of it from the last parking area on the paved part of the road to NIEDERTHEI. The Oetztal claims another "highest" at its southern end: **Obergurgl.** No other Austrian village with a church stands higher than this cosy little resort (6,320 ft. or 1,922 m.).

If you have a taste for summer skiing, take the cable car or a winding mountain road from SÖLDEN to the Retenbachferner.

Monuments from the old days: Oetztal inn and pensive customer.

North-East Tyrol

The chic resort of Kitzbühel is the kingpin of the region, which also embraces the dramatic landscapes of the Kaisergebirge and the chief towns of the Unterinntal or Lower Inn Valley: medieval Rattenberg and Brixlegg, graced with three venerable castles.

Kitzbühel

If fame depends on history books, then Innsbruck is of course Tyrol's most important town. But if you get your history from the newspapers, Kitzbühel undoubtedly takes first place. Not only winter sports events like the world-famous Hahnenkamm race and the smart life of *après-ski,* but also the relaxed pleasures of summer chalets and the town's idyllic surroundings have made Kitzbühel—or "Kitz"—the darling of the Beautiful People.

As a tourist attraction in the 19th century, Kitzbühel first appealed to the older set as a spa resort because of the warm waters and healing mud of the Schwarzsee, the lake on the north-west edge of town. Only at the end of the century, with the introduction of skiing from Norway, did the younger crowd move in. Today, the Schwarzsee is a magnet for family bathers, while providing cures for slipped discs of all ages. And the exhilarating sports of climbing and hiking in the summer supplement winter skiing to give the town all-round appeal.

Kitzbühel's particular flavour probably derives from its charmed situation: the town looks north to the formidable, jagged peaks of the aptly named Wilder Kaiser mountains from a cosy valley at the foot of the more inviting Kitzbüheler Alps. This juxtaposition of fierce and serene landscapes seems to give life here a unique lift.

Miraculously, the 700-year-old town has been spared the tragic upheavals and wars of Tyrolean history. Kitzbühel enjoys a quiet prosperity which achieved its first boom during the 16th-century exploitation of the silver mines before capitalizing on the present-day gold mine of tourism.

By the stream of the Kitzbüheler Ache, the old inner town retains the oval form traced by long-vanished—and happily superfluous—medieval ramparts. The graceful houses with their overhanging gable roofs divide into just two parallel streets: the Vorderstadt, closer to the river, and the Hinterstadt. At the southern end

Kitzbühel's fairy-tale atmosphere mixes with modern sophistication.

stands the 16th-century tower of the Pfleghof, on the site of the castle occupied by the town's guardian in the days when Kitzbühel belonged to the Bavarians. Immediately west of the tower is a granary that now houses an amusing **folklore museum** *(Heimatmuseum)*. Littered with fascinating memorabilia from the mining era, the ground floor has the appearance of a merry little junkshop. On the upper two floors, arranged in more respectful order, are displays of prehistoric mining implements and more recent paraphernalia illustrating the complete history of skiing, from the wooden planks in use in the 1890s to the streamlined fibre-glass wonders of today. This is one place where you can't get away from the fact that 1956 Olympic triple gold-medal winner Toni Sailer, second in Tyrolean esteem only to freedom-fighter Andreas Hofer, was a Kitzbühel boy. His equipment is on exhibit.

Along the Hinterstadt, you'll see some of the best of the town's older houses. The regional police headquarters *(Bezirkshauptmannschaft)* at No. 28–30, once the offices of an important trading firm, has a beautiful Renaissance arcaded gallery on the inner courtyard and a peaceful little garden at the rear, shaded by maples and pine trees. Take a look, too, at the venerable hostelry of the Goldener Greif.

Two churches stand together on a mound north of the old city limits. **Pfarrkirche St. Andreas,** the larger of the two churches, was built in the 15th century but transformed in Baroque style in 1785 by the renowned Kitzbühel architect Andrä Huber. The damage of over-zealous restoration in

Fremdenverkehrsverband Kitzbühel

1896 has been largely repaired to provide a more tasteful setting for the works of the Faistenberger family, a dynasty of local artists. The black-and-gold 17th-century altar is by sculptor Benedikt, while the paintings of the Magi on the south wall and the Crucifixion on the organ loft are 18th-century works by Simon Benedikt. Take a look, too, at the delicately carved 18th-century choir stalls of Franz Offer.

The **Liebfrauenkirche,** endowed with a massive bell tower, is in its interior a more intimate edifice, divided into two chapels. The lower chapel is 14th-century, the upper Baroque, glowing with Simon Benedikt Faistenberger's Madonna frescoes and ornamented with two masterpieces of wrought ironwork—the florid entrance grill and the rose gate in front of the altar.

For a break from sightseeing, go out for a swim in the **Schwarzsee,** a pleasant 15-minute walk. The water is amazingly warm for the altitude, around 2,600 feet (800 m.)—it's something in the mud. Mud baths are highly recommended for every imaginable ache and pain, particularly after a long walk over the meadows on the **Hahnenkamm** or **Kitzbüheler Horn.** These mountain heights are by no means reserved for winter skiing. Cable cars go up in summer, providing a head start for easy, 2½-hour walks: to the Ehrenbachhöhe, the alpine meadow on the Hahnenkamm, or to the Bichlalm from the Kitzbüheler Horn. Take a picnic or eat a hearty snack on the way at a rustic snack bar or Jausenstation (see p.99).

At the foot of the Horn, in Hinterobernau, is the enchanting **Tiroler Bauernhausmuseum,** a huge farm house refitted with furniture, cooking utensils and farm implements.

Around Kitzbühel

One of the prettiest excursions is the half-hour drive south through the forests of the Kitzbüheler Alps to **Pass Thurn** (leading to the Pinzgau district in the province of Salzburg). Stop off at **Aurach** to visit the nature park. A marked road guides you through this reserve to watch the grazing and, in season, wooing and mating of rare species of deer, goat and wild boar, strictly for looking, not hunting. At JOCHBERG you can see traces of old-time copper and silver mining in the grassed-over slag heaps at the side of the road. In the hills east of town, a marked path twists through dense forest and across makeshift, but perfectly safe, bridges and fords to the beautiful **Sintersbacher Waterfall.**

The **Brixental** (west of Kitzbühel) provides a gentle contrast to Pass Thurn's dramatic vistas. In this valley all is sweetness and light: gingerbread houses in **Kirchberg,** the elegant Mariä Himmelfahrt parish church of **Brixen im Thale**—a beautiful cable-car ride up to Hohe Salve for a great view—and the medieval market town of **Hopfgarten.**

St. Johann in Tirol

At the confluence of three alpine streams, the Reither, Kitzbüheler and Pillerseer Ache, St. Johann in Tirol provides an easy-going, family-oriented complement to sophisticated "Kitz". One of the region's most popular summer resorts, it offers a wealth of sport and leisure facilities in col-

Timber industry is important to the economy of north-east Tyrol.

ourful, sympathetic surroundings within easy reach of lazy promenades along the river or more strenuous hikes in the Kaisergebirge to the northwest.

Many of the massive, gable-roofed houses are painted around the windows with brightly coloured arabesques or over the doorways with religious portraits in the Bavarian *Lüftlmalerei* (façade painting) tradition. The **Gasthof zum Bären**—one of the Tyrol's most famous hostelries in a region where inns have always been of historical importance—served as headquarters for Josef Speckbacher, leader of north Tyrolean operations in the 1809 uprising.

Entirely in keeping with St. Johann's cheerful atmosphere, the 18th-century parish church, **Mariä Himmelfahrt,** has a bold, inviting façade. Bell-shaped domes cap the western towers. The pink-and-yellow interior displays some forceful frescoes by the prolific Simon Benedikt Faistenberger, most importantly *Mary and the Holy Trinity* over the choir. On the western outskirts of town, the much older **Spitalkirche** is worth a visit for the fine 15th-century stained-glass window behind the high altar. This portrayal of ten saints is the only Gothic stained-glass window to survive in the Austrian Tyrol. For good measure, the church's 700-year-old bell is the oldest in the province.

The **Pillerseetal,** a short drive east of St. Johann, is a narrow winding valley where towering cliffs form spectacular granite pillars on the eastern slopes, the beginning of the Loferer Steinberge. Down below, a lake scarcely more than pond-size offers pleasant windsurfing and rowing among the reeds. **St. Jakob in Haus** is the valley's principal village, a popular refuge for merchants and pilgrims

How You Gonna Keep 'em Down on the Farm...?

For centuries, whenever their cattle were threatened by disease, Tyrolean peasants have made a pilgrimage to the chapel of St. Adolari, the saintly protector of cattle, to pray for deliverance. In the 1780s, the enlightened, reform-minded Emperor Joseph II tried to put a stop to this "superstitious" practice. But the peasants kept on coming and to this day, disease or not, cattle herders come to pray at St. Adolari every month of May.

Litter must be a capital crime in the spotless village of Waidring.

who ever since the Middle Ages have lit a candle at the portrait of St. Jakob (James), the traveller's patron saint. At the southern tip of the Piller See is the onion-domed parish church of St. Ulrich.

The valley's architectural jewel lies at the other end of the lake: the tiny church of **St. Adolari,** a pilgrimage chapel built in 1407. In 1957, restorers uncovered the lovely Gothic Madonna frescoes on the choir walls.

Immediately north of the Pillerseetal, **Waidring** is one of those idyllic little villages—flowers spilling over the balconies, windows ornamented with the most delicate *Lüftlmalerei* motifs—that affects even the most unsentimental traveller. It snuggles up to the comforting and solid Baroque parish church, **St. Veit,** which boasts a fine canopied altar by Josef Martin Lengauer. Some 7 kilometres further west, Erpfendorf proves interesting for its modern

20th-century church, **St. Barbara,** by Clemens Holzmeister. The paintings in the interior make a fascinatingly cinematic impact, presenting the *Stations of the Cross* as a series of "close-ups".

Kaisergebirge

Literally "the Emperor's mountain range", probably by dint of medieval feudal rights exercised by the Holy Roman Emperor over mountain lands, the mighty Kaisergebirge has a majestic splendour all its own. Most of it is a national nature reserve. The range includes not the tallest but certainly the most rugged mountains in the Tyrol, a constant challenge to seasoned climbers. These form the Wilder Kaiser, curving south-east from Kufstein. But the mountains of the "tame" Zahmer Kaiser to the north-east are easily accessible to hikers—and any of us lesser mortals who just like to get away from civilization without risking our necks. A shallow valley, the Kaisertal, separates the wild heights from the tame. Here, in Tischofer Cave, were discovered the earliest traces of human settlement in the Tyrol. The Kaisergebirge is surrounded by hospitable resorts that make ideal bases for mountain explorations.

Kufstein

The town's situation high above the east bank of the River Inn is as picturesque as any in the Tyrol, but the first thing you see is the grim fortifications of **Festung Kufstein,** surmounted by a massive round tower *(Kaiserturm).* It's also practically the *last* thing

Kufstein deserves a little rest after all those devastating wars.

remaining from the town's troubled past as a punching bag in the historic power struggles between Bavarians and Austrians. (Kufstein was devastated in four major conflicts: Maximilian's victory over the Bavarians in 1504, the War of the Spanish Succession in 1703, the Napoleonic Wars, 1809, and the Allied bombardments of 1944.) Climb up—or take the lift—to the towers and battlements on the granite cliffs and you'll see why kings and emperors coveted this strategic location. The defences command the river at the western edge of the formidable natural fortress constituted by the Kaisergebirge. The **views** of the Inn valley and of the Wilder Kaiser are truly magnificent.

After all the turmoil, the castle today shelters the blessedly peaceful **folklore museum** *(Heimatmuseum)* notable for exhibits of finds made by archaeologists in Tischofer Cave in 1906, excavations which prompted the museum's foundation. Highlights include skeletal remains of gigantic bears from 30,000 B.C. (very possibly hunted in the Kaisertal by the Tyrol's earliest inhabitants), implements from Stone Age settlements, and Bronze Age mining equipment, which anticipated the first major source of subsequent Tyrolean prosperity. Other exhibits illustrate Kufstein's dramatic history.

In the castle's Neuhof courtyard, you can hear organ recitals at midday (also at 6 p.m. in the summer months) on the huge Heldenorgel, a monument to the fallen heroes of World War I. Housed in the Bürgerturm, this organ has no less than 4,307 pipes, 46 stops and 30 bells, making it, according to town fathers, the largest free-standing organ in the world. Two enormous cables link the organ to the keyboard, in a pavilion in the Festungshof, 262 feet (80 m.) below.

Kufstein's liveliest and most attractive street is the **Römerhofgasse,** where you'll find the best of the old taverns.

Quite apart from the ravages of war, successive Baroque, Neoclassical and modern restorations have left the parish church, **St. Veit,** with little of its original 15th-century decoration—all the more reason to notice the superbly sculpted old tombstones of Kufstein's leading citizens, set in the south wall. One in particular has a nicely gruesome "before and after" touch: mining magnate Hans Paumgartner is portrayed in his prime and as a corpse half-eaten away by worms, with the inscription: "Rich and poor, we all end up like this".

The surrounding countryside abounds in splendid walking opportunities. An unhurried, four-hour ramble due east of town into the **Kaisertal** takes you past Tischofer Cave, 196 feet (60 m.) deep, 65 feet (20 m.) wide, and on to red-roofed Antonius-Kapelle—a perfect introduction to the diverse landscapes of the Kaisergebirge. From the west bank of the River Inn, go for a leisurely three-hour hike to four warm-water **lakes:** the Pfrillsee, Längsee, Hechtsee (best for family swimming) and Egelsee.

Kaisergebirge Tour

A drive of 85 kilometres takes you completely around the Kaisergebirge, an entertaining excursion ideally done as a two-day outing with an overnight stay at one of the little villages along the route.

Setting out north of Kufstein, the first stop is **Ebbs.** In this land of Baroque, the parish church, **Unserer Lieben Frau Geburt,** is notable for the pleasing simplicity of the interior. No fussy stuccowork detracts from Josef Adam Mölk's trompe l'oeil ceiling frescoes, or from the fine sculptures of the 12 apostles by Josef Martin Lengauer, who also designed the high altar framing a lovely Gothic Madonna. A major attraction for children and adults alike is the **Ebbser Fohlenhof,** stables and riding establishment, where the world-renowned Haflinger horses, originally from Merano in South Tyrol, are bred from European and Arab stock. You can attend riding shows or take a trip through the surrounding countryside in a coach or open gig.

At the sleepy village of NIEDERNDORF, turn east towards **Walchsee**, a major resort for sailing, windsurfing, trout fishing or swimming (lake waters register temperatures of 75 °F or 24 °C in summer).

Kössen commands the northeast corner of the Kaisergebirge, and its old houses boast some of the finest *Lüftlmalerei* decoration in the Tyrol. The painting on the late Gothic Gasthof Erzherzog Rainer is especially attractive. Around here, hikers make for the tranquil blue Taubensee, a lake on the German-Austrian border. (Allow two hours for the walk.) Sportsmen enjoy canoeing on the swift-flowing Kössener Ache.

The southbound road follows this stream past St. Johann (see p. 63) and turns west

via GOING, a dreamy hamlet on a babbling brook, to the lively resort of ELLMAU. Further on, at SCHEFFAU, take the side road north 5 kilometres to the serenely beautiful **Hintersteiner See.** There are few sights more romantic than the clear waters of this secluded lake at sunset, bordered by mountain elms and larches against the stark backdrop of the Wilder Kaiser.

Wildschönau

This plateau at the end of a valley winding south and then west from the important railway town of WÖRGL is quite simply a paradise for nature lovers. Even the most hardened city-slicker will succumb to the wonderful spring and summer displays of meadow flowers—primroses, crocuses, wild marigolds, anemones and, the higher you go, sweet-smelling heaths of rosemary and alpine azaleas. In season, you can pick the wild bilberries (whortleberries). Watch out for wild goats, a fox or two, marten, polecat, even badger. Stop at a farmhouse to sample the fragrant honey that the Wildschönau bees concoct from

Nearly one o'clock, time to knock off and swap a yarn with his pals.

alpine roses. Refresh yourself with the wine they make from juniper berries or, if you need to warm up, try the local *Krautler*—a pungent spirit distilled from turnips.

Oberau, chief village of the valley, is distinguished by the striking bell tower with three green bulb domes of the parish church, **St. Margaretha.** True believers light a candle on the altar before setting off on hikes—Margaretha being the patron saint of wanderers in the wilderness. MÜHLTHAL and AUFFACH are the favoured starting points for those nature walks. Take a deep breath and a picnic, and away you go.

Unterinntal

(Lower Inn Valley)

North of the River Inn, drive up into the hills and on through dense forest to **Mariastein,** site of a fortress built by the fighting Freundsberg knights to guard the Inn valley in the 14th century. Atop the tower is the Gnadenkapelle (Chapel of Mercy), with its beautifully carved Gothic *Madonna and Child*. On your way up to the chapel, notice the angels' heads set in the roof of the spiral staircase.

The road south-west of Wörgl takes you beyond KUNDL to the church of **St. Leonhard auf der Wiese,**

dedicated to the patron saint of miners. The 15th-century edifice is a handsome example of sober late Gothic design; restrained Baroque altars were added later. There's a splendid stone sculpture (1481) of Leonhard, who looks tough enough to have been a miner himself. Note, too, the nicely carved lions ornamenting the pews.

Rattenberg is one of the prettiest towns in the Tyrol. Lining the main street are medieval houses painted russet, dove grey, ochre and pink, many of them embellished with graceful gable windows, arched doorways of red marble and intricate, wrought-iron tavern signs or coats-of-arms. Park your car on the edge of town (traffic is banned from the centre) and wander back into the Middle Ages. Don't worry, it's not far. Rattenberg is, with 600 inhabitants, the smallest fully fledged town in the province.

Despite its size, Rattenberg has played an important role in Tyrolean history. Its strategic location on the river made it a prized Bavarian possession, along with Kufstein and Kitzbühel. Subsequently Rattenberg prospered as a partner in the Tyrol mining industry, and the wealth of the town was supplemented by glass works dating back to the 17th century. The **glass workshops** off the main street remain a major tourist attraction today. The direct inspiration for the double church at Schwaz, **St. Virgil** achieved a happy architectural harmony in its two naves and two choirs for separate congregations of merchants and miners. The airy stuccowork of Anton Gigl provides the perfect counterpart to the exuberant frescoes of Simon Benedikt Faistenberger and Matthäus Günther.

Take time out for a moment of peaceful meditation beside the river in the Gothic cloisters of the **Servitenkirche** dedicated to St. Augustine. And, for an overall view of the town in its riverside setting, walk up to the ruin of the 14th-century **castle** *(Burg).*

Across the river in **Kramsach** you might like to visit one of the most dubious museums in the world, the **Musterfriedhof** (literally "model cemetery"), where a local smith displays his private collection of bizarre inscriptions found in the region. A sample from among the least outrageous: *Here in this pit, Two miller-*

Rattenberg is always a bustling town, especially at holiday time.

SPARKASSE
Käse

boys sit, Born on Chiem Lake, Died of belly-ache.

East of Kramsach are five lovely little lakes for swimming and other water sports. Kramsach itself stands at the beginning of the exquisite **Brandenbergertal,** a valley which originates dramatically in the rugged Rofan mountains—in summer, rubber raft races are held in the torrent down below—and levels out in a gentle landscape of green meadows and venerable farmhouses, where they make time-honoured *Prügeltorte* (cudgel cake, see p. 102).

Back on the south bank of the Inn, **Brixlegg** boasts three medieval **castles,** all on the western outskirts: Burg Matzen and Burg Lichtenwerth, both set in charming parks and much renovated and centrally heated, and Burg Kropfsberg, lying in romantic ruins. None of them was really forbidding—they were cosy piles in which the occupants could sit and wait for the enemy to go away.

Sophisticated and modern, the elegant mountain resort of **Alpbach** stands at the far end of the delightful valley bearing its name. Host to the famous summer seminars of the European Forum, the town also provides relaxation for tired brains with invigorating walks through the mountains.

East Tyrol

Geographically isolated in 1919 when the region south of the Brenner Pass was ceded to Italy, East Tyrol is now the province's southernmost area. The climate is noticeably warmer, especially in the Pustertal, while palm trees flourish in the capital, Lienz. The province of Salzburg separates it from the rest of Tyrol, but its relative remoteness—considerably shortened now by the Felbertauern Tunnel—has meant that its landscapes have kept a pristine freshness of their own.

Lienz

The liveliest spot in this easy-going, unpretentious town is **Hauptplatz,** where the brightly painted façades, open-air cafés and jolly, pink-domed police headquarters and courthouse create the atmosphere of a Mediterranean piazza.

At the western edge of town, on a tree-covered slope, rises **Schloss Bruck,** seat of the Görz dynasty from whom Emperor Maximilian took over the government of East Tyrol in 1500. After serving variously as a convent, an arsenal, a military hospital, a brewery and a tavern, the castle now houses the Bezirksmuseum (regional museum). It's well worth a visit,

The piazza palm trees of Lienz are unmistakably Mediterranean.

not only for the fine collection of regional furniture and costumes, but also for the paintings by Franz von Defregger, Josef Steiner and Karl Anrather, whose portraiture gives a striking impression of the peasant faces you'll encounter today in the surrounding valleys. A separate gallery is devoted to the works of East Tyrol's most revered painter, Albin Egger-Lienz (1868–1926), a Tyrolean counterpart to Switzerland's Ferdinand Hodler. His treatment of historical subjects and peasant life manages to be at once sentimental and brutal. You'll find a gentle antidote in the castle's **Dreifaltigkeitskapelle,** a charming Romanesque-Gothic chapel on two levels. There's an almost primitive simplicity to the Görzer Altar of 1500 in the lower room.

EAST TYROL
0 5 10 km
0 5 10 miles
WEST GERMANY
MÜNCHEN
Ainring
SALZBURG
KLAGENFURT
Bad Reichenhall
Hallein
Salzach
Kössen
Reit im Winkl
Niederndorf
Walchsee
Ebbs
Walchsee
Kössener Ache
Kiefersfelden
Thiersee
Zahmer Kaiser
Kaisergebirge
Kufstein
Wilder Kaiser
Erpfendorf
Waidring
Lofer
Bischofswiesen
Ramsau
Berchtesgaden
Hintersee
Königssee
Mariastein
Hintersteiner See
Scheffau
St. Johann i. T.
Pillerseetal
Piller See
Loferer-
Steinberge
INNSBRUCK
Inn
Elmau
Going
St. Jakob i. H.
Wörgl
Hohe Salve 1827
Kitzbüheler Horn 1998
Oberau
Brixen
Schwarzsee
Bichlalm
Mühlthal
Hopfgarten
Kirchberg
Kitzbühel
Bichl
Aurach
Piller-See-Ache
Saalfelden
Leogang
Auffach
1655 Hahnenkamm
Wildschönau
Saalbach
Jochberg
Hinterglemm
Kitzbüheler Alpen
Zell am See
Zeller See
Jochbergwald
Pass Thurn
1274
Uttendorf
Bruck
Walchen
Mittersill
Salzach
Salzach
Gerlos
Krimml
Fusch
Rauris
Blessachkogel 3050
G. Wiessbachhorn 3564
Reichensp. 3303
Gr. Venediger 3674
Felbertauerntunnel
Badgastein
Dreiherrnspitze 3499
Eicham 3371
Grossglockner 3794
Hoher Sonnblick 3105
Luckner-H.
Obermauer
Hinterbichl
Virgen
Matrei i. O.
Kals
Heiligenblut
VIRGENTAL
Ganz
OSTTIROL
Kalser Tal
Petzeck 3283
Collalto Hochgall 3436
Erlsbach
St. Veit i. D.
Hopfgarten i. Defereggen
St. Jakob i. D.
2055 Stallersattel
DEFEREGGENTAL
ITALY
Winklern
1204
Iselsberg
Aguntum
Deferegger Alpen
LIENZ
Dölsach
Kreuzeck 2702
N
St. Justina
Thal
Amlach
Lavant
Heinfels
PUSTERTAL
Drau
Oberdrauburg
Sillian
Dobbiaco
S. Candido
Kartitsch

Pfarrkirche St. Andrä (St. Andrew's Parish Church) is built on Romanesque foundations. The sober white Gothic edifice preserves some interesting decorative elements: carved Romanesque lions in the entrance hall, a high Gothic *Pietà* in the crypt, late Gothic wall paintings and Baroque frescoes in the choir. In the former cemetery, a memorial to the victims of World War I has frescoes by Egger-Lienz, who is himself buried here.

The excavated Roman town of **Aguntum,** an important outpost of the empire until its destruction by Germanic tribes in the 7th century A.D., is just 4 kilometres east of Lienz on the road to DÖLSACH. Archaeologists have uncovered the remains of the main city gate, an atrium house, metal foundry, and baths with elaborate central-heating system. A museum on the site provides an essential explanation of what might otherwise just look like—what they are—some very old walls and columns. A couple of kilometres further south are the 5th-century remains of the bishopric of **Lavant.** On a hill adjoining the site is the parish church. Higher up, the 15th-century St. Peter and Paul church rises on the foundations of an early Christian baptistery.

Pustertal

This sunny valley linking Lienz to Italy is best reached by way of the **Pustertaler Höhenstrasse,** a mountain road which offers panoramas of the Lienzer Dolomites.

Take the Höhenstrasse from **Thal,** dominated by the noble spire of its Gothic church, St. Korbinian. The late 15th-century altar paintings, especially the one of Mary Magdalene, are a powerful product of the distinctive Pustertal School led by the Pacher family. It's worth making the short climb by foot up to the tiny hamlet of **St. Justina,** notable for Friedrich Pacher's altar paintings. But above all you'll enjoy the valley's natural beauties, contrasting with the starkness of the Dolomites to the south.

At **Heinfels,** take a look at the half-ruined medieval castle that sprawls across a grassy mound. Unlike those Tyrolean piles that resemble one big block house, this is a *real* castle, the kind you might have built in your playroom.

Sillian, the Pustertal's principal resort, proves very popular with skiers in the winter and hikers and fishermen in the summer. The medieval origins of this old market town are recalled by the pillory in the main square.

Kalser Tal

This pretty little valley 20 kilometres north of Lienz offers a close-up view of one of Austria's great natural wonders: the **Grossglockner,** highest mountain in the country at 12,454 feet (3,797 m.). The mountain actually lies across the provincial border in Carinthia, but the Tyrolean approach is a favourite with hikers.

Just north of the village of KALS, a toll road ascends to the Luckner-Haus, a hostelry from

Kalser Tal is a hiker's paradise—it's heaven for sun-bathers, too.

which you start out on a leisurely walk to various viewing points up the mountain. Each stop has a very welcome restaurant to sustain you for the next stage of your journey, further up or back down, depending on your endurance. Experienced hikers make it to 9,190 feet (2,802 m.) above sea level, to the Stüdlhütte, while the real climbers stop off at the Erzherzog-Johann-Hütte, at 11,329 feet (3,454 m.) the highest chalet in Austria, before tackling the summit. Lesser mortals can enjoy the splendid Grossglockner spectacle from the Luckner-Hütte, 7,271 feet (2,217 m.) high, an easy 45-minute walk from the inn.

Defereggental

On the west side of the Felberntauernstrasse, the main route to Lienz, this broad and bright valley offers wonderfully peaceful moments off the beaten track in the mountain villages of **Hopfgarten** and **St. Veit,** surrounded by sunny alpine meadows and dense pine forests.

Chief resort is **St. Jakob** —good fishing and guided hiking tours on the higher paths—gateway to the meandering, and in this case literally breath-taking, mountain road over the 6,730-foot (2,052-m.) Staller Sattel into Italy.

Virgental

Matrei, the gateway to the Virgental, traces its history back to the Bronze Age. It thrived as an important trading centre in the Middle Ages, when it was guarded by Schloss Weissenstein. The castle stands in dignified ruin north of town, since it was struck by a lightning bolt in 1962. The Baroque church of **St. Alban** retains its Gothic steeple. Decoration includes some imposing ceiling frescoes by Franz Anton Zeiller, most notably *The Miracle of the Loaves and the Fishes,* covering the length of the nave.

Be sure to seek out **St. Nicolas** *(Nikolauskirche),* a Romanesque-Gothic treasure just south-west of Matrei on a hill above the hamlet of GANZ. (Ask for the key at house number 15 in Ganz itself.) This 12th-century fortress-church with a double choir, one over the other, has frescoes of Adam and Eve, Jacob's Ladder, and the Apostles.

The valley road climbs up the northern slopes high over the River Isel, through a serene landscape of larch forests and emerald meadows. If the weather's good, leave your car at the cheerful resort town of **Virgen** and take a pleasant 90-minute walk along clearly marked forest paths up to the castle-

Madonna and mountain climbers are portrayed on a roadside shrine.

ruins of Rabenstein and beyond it to **Allerheiligenkapelle** (All Saints' Chapel), carved from rock on the site of a pagan temple. This is the perfect place to commune with nature and entertain a pagan thought or two of your own before returning to Virgen for at least a beer or apple juice at the turreted, 16th-century tavern.

In a valley unusually rich in architectural gems, a masterpiece awaits you at **Obermauer.** High above the river, the 15th-century Gothic **pilgrimage church** *(Zu Unserer Lieben Frau vom Schnee)* stands on a weathered stone platform framed by some splendid, darktimbered houses. The setting is a pure joy. Notice the reliefs from an older edifice set in the outside walls, particularly an *Adoration of the Magi* on the south side. The

interior is magnificently decorated with late Gothic frescoes by Simon von Taisten in the poignant style of the Pustertaler School. These simply presented scenes of the Passion (above the nave) and the life of the Virgin, to whom the church is dedicated (in the choir), together with the quiet dignity of the pulpit and the sculpture on the altars, contrast eloquently with the lavish Baroque decoration prevailing in most Tyrolean churches.

Excursions

You don't have to be a bomb-throwing extremist contesting Italy's right to South Tyrol to feel that the German-speaking portion of the alpine province of Alto Adige is still an important part of Austrian Tyrol's cultural reality. A visit, at least to the historic centres of Merano and Bolzano and their environs, reveals the many affinities of the area with the Tyrol north of the Brenner Pass—as well as the undeniable differences.

Unlike South Tyrol, there's no historical excuse for including an excursion to Salzburg in a Tyrolean holiday. But this golden city, home of Mozart and a thousand other musical dreams, needs no excuse when the *Autobahn* brings it so close to Kufstein or Kitzbühel.

South Tyrol

The architecture of the houses and churches, the traditional costumes of the peasants, the cuisine, the mixture of piety and robust rural humour will all remind you of the Austrian Tyrol. And yet, as was always the case, no amount of German-language street signs and newspapers or *Apfelstrudel* can gainsay the fact that the vineyards, the first few cypress trees, the warmer spring and hotter summer all bespeak the presence of Italy. The Mediterranean is that much closer on these southern slopes of the Alps.

Merano *(Meran)*

After it lost the status of Tyrolean capital to Innsbruck in 1420, and then the mint to Hall, Merano fell into oblivion. By the 18th century, cattle were roaming the city centre. In 1836, a Viennese court doctor, Josef Huber, informed his royal patients that Merano's climate and its table grapes had great healing properties, turning the dilapidated town almost overnight into a thriving spa frequented by the crowned heads of Europe.

Like them, you can stroll along the **Summer** and **Winter Promenades** *(Passeggiata d'Estate* and *d'Inverno)* on the banks of the swift River Passirio. Copper beeches, chestnuts and fir trees cast their shade, but there are cypresses, too—a reminder that Tuscany is near at hand. The statue of "Sissy", wife of Austrian Emperor Franz Joseph, which graces the Summer Promenade, recalls the Habsburgs. Open-air concerts of Strauss waltzes are held in front of the gleaming yellow-and-white Kursaal, a public hall built in 1914.

Though the crowned heads have gone, the tourist business thrives, nowhere more than in the arcaded **Laubengasse** *(Via dei Portici),* an elegant shopping centre. At the eastern end is the **Cathedral** *(Duomo),* an imposing late Gothic structure. Two finely sculpted stone porches project from the southern wall. The octagonal Barbara Chapel beside the choir boasts a Rhenish Gothic altar triptych (bought from an antique dealer and installed in 1911), flanked on either side by massive Baroque altars.

A stairway north of the church leads to **Passeggiata Tappeiner**. The promenade winds among cypresses, palms and vines to the top of a little hill for a superb **view** of the whole town.

North of Merano, the **Val Passiria** *(Passeiertal)* offers pleasant drives up to 12th-century Schloss Tirol, fortress of Tyrol's medieval dukes, and then from RIFIANO *(Riffian),* with its pilgrimage church to S. LEONARDO *(St. Leonhard),* where Tyrolean hero Andreas Hofer was born in the local inn, Gasthof zum Sandwirt.

Bolzano *(Bozen)*
The lively commercial capital of Alto Adige provides a shopping mecca for people touring South Tyrol. Bolzano has its own smart version of the characteristically Tyrolean arcade, the **Laubengasse** *(Via dei Portici),* north of Waltherplatz *(Piazza Walther)* in the city centre. Summer concerts are held on this square amid elegant open-air cafés—attractively canopied on the hottest days—which look across to the towering **Cathedral** *(Duomo).* The 14th-and 15th-century Romanesque-Gothic church has a polychrome tiled roof reminiscent of Vienna's St. Stephen's Cathedral and a three-tiered belfry, 213 feet (65 m.) high. The interior, badly damaged in World War II, contains a miraculously preserved sandstone **pulpit** of 1514, with fine reliefs of the Fathers of the Church, sculpted by Hans Lutz von Schussenried.

West of Waltherplatz lies the **Dominican Convent** *(Convento dei Domenicani),* which nowadays houses the Academy of Music. Don't miss **St. John's Chapel** in the Dominican church, decorated with beautiful

Time out to read the newspaper on Merano's summer promenade.

KOFLER

14th-century frescoes. These biblical scenes, including a dramatic *Apocalypse,* were painted by disciples of Giotto engaged by a rich Florentine banking family that had settled in Bolzano.

Bolzano's environs are rich in hiking opportunities and magnificent views of the Dolomites: best of all is the **panorama** from the Renon *(Ritten)* plateau, around the charming village of COLLALBO *(Klobenstein).*

Salzburg

Since Salzburg offers one of Europe's great urban panoramas, start with an overall view by taking the lift from Gstättengasse up to the terrace of Café Winkler on the **Mönchsberg.** Stroll across to the halfway-station of the funicular railway and go up to **Hohensalzburg,** the archbishops' castle, for a look at the princely life led by Salzburg's aristocratic churchmen. You'll see from the massive walls and towers and dungeons that the castle was a fortress bristling with military defences, rather than a palatial retreat for spiritual meditation.

Bolzano's summer heat makes watermelon a welcome treat.

The Salzburg archbishops were rarely popular enough to overcome the fear of civic rebellion.

Guided tours visit the elegant 16th-century Princes' rooms *(Fürstenzimmer)* on the third and fourth floors of the Hoher Stock, noted for the splendour of its intricate late Gothic decoration. One of the highlights is the Golden Room *(Goldene Stube),* with its magnificent monumental ceramic tiled stove, each polychrome panel illustrating a scene from the Scriptures. The castle museum has a first-class collection of medieval sculpture; also on display are the weapons and instruments of torture used to bolster the archbishops' power.

Back down the Mönchsberg, at the foot of the funicular railway, stands **St. Peterskirche** (St. Peter's Church), richly remodelled in the Baroque style with red and white Salzburg marble. The **cemetery,** shaded by pines and weeping willows, is the elegant, even romantic, resting place of Salzburg's noblest families, including the Trapps of "Sound of Music" fame—not everything in this town is by Mozart.

The nearby **Franziskanerkirche,** a late Romanesque convent church, has a Gothic steeple. The nave, a model of sobriety, is lightened by the bright Gothic choir. The grand, golden Baroque high altar by the Viennese architect Johann Bernhard Fischer von Erlach frames a poignant 15th-century *Madonna* (the Christ on her lap was added in 1895) by the Tyrol's finest sculptor and painter, Michael Pacher.

Walk past the Festspielhaus to Sigmundsplatz and the **Pferdeschwemme,** a horse trough to end all horse troughs. This grandiose Renaissance struc-

The Church of the Franciscans is just one of Salzburg's splendours.

ture is ornamented with vigorous sculpture and frescoes of prancing horses.

Kollegienkirche (University Church) figures among the masterpieces of Fischer von Erlach's Baroque architecture. The powerful, twin-towered façade on Universitätsplatz presents an imposing frame for

the massive dome looming behind it.

Getreidegasse is *the* great shopping street of Salzburg's old town. Wrought-iron guild signs ornament its Renaissance and Baroque façades. At number 9 is **Mozart's birthplace**—the great event took place on January 27, 1756—now an enchanting museum. This is where the little tyke knocked out his first sonatas; you can see the child-size fiddle he played them on. Exhibits include manuscripts of minuets Mozart wrote when he was five, his counterpoint notebook, paintings of papa Leopold and sister Nannerl. A clavichord bears a note written by wife Constanza: "On this piano my dearly departed husband Mozart composed the Magic Flute".

The early 17th-century **Residenz,** another palace of the archbishops, now serves as an art gallery. The excellent collection of Flemish and Dutch paintings includes a Rembrandt portrait of his mother at prayer, a Rubens portrait of Emperor Charles V and superb landscapes by Jan van Goyen and Jacob van Ruisdael.

The south side of the Residenzplatz is dominated by the huge **Dom** (Cathedral).

In keeping with the ambitious visions of Salzburg's archbishops, Wolf Dietrich von Raitenau commissioned a church bigger than St. Peter's in Rome. But he was forced out of office at the beginning of the 17th century, before his project could be realized. Today's edifice, executed in Italian Renaissance style (with Baroque overtones) is certainly imposing enough. In the first chapel on the left as you enter is a bronze baptismal font in which, on January 28, 1756, a little chappy was christened Johann Chrysostomus Wolfgang Theophil Mozart, later shortened to Wolfgang Amadeus.

Have a pastry in one of the cafés on **Mozartplatz**—or the deadly sweet local version of a soufflé, *Salzburger Nockerl*—and watch the world go by.

Beyond Salzburg lies the blessedly tranquil **Fuschlsee.** At the west end of this crystal-clear lake—no motor boots allowed—is Schloss Fuschl, once the castle-home of Nazi Foreign Minister Joachim von Ribbentrop, now a respectable hotel.

The Festival

The Salzburg Festival, the Mozartian counterpart to Bayreuth's homage to Wagner, is held from the end of July to the end of August. Founded in 1920, this feast of opera, symphony concerts and chamber music recitals is dominated by, but not exclusively devoted to, Mozart. Customarily the proceedings begin with an open-air production of Hugo von Hoffmannsthal's *Jedermann* (Everyman), following a tradition established by Max Reinhardt, the great theatre director and co-founder of the festival.

Since Furtwängler and Toscanini in the 1930s, the greatest artists in the world have considered it a supreme privilege to perform at the Salzburg Festival. It's almost as great a privilege to get tickets. Reservations can be made from the end of November; by the beginning of January, there's very little left. A travel agency or the Austrian National Tourist Office can help you apply.

Your best bet is to aim for the second half of August, when the premières are over and all the honorary guests and journalists have left town. Be sure to couple ticket reservations with a hotel room, since festival regulars bag most of the available space a year in advance. Even if the most popular events are sold out, you can usually find tickets for recitals or chamber concerts, all well worthwhile.

What to Do

Sports

Tyroleans have a very sane attitude to sport: they enjoy it immensely, get a lot of fun out of it and take it very, very seriously. Whatever sports you choose to pursue here, be sure to bring the proper equipment. What you don't already have, you can purchase locally in the excellent sports shops. Amid beautiful landscapes in this most bracing of climates, you'll find sport an aesthetic delight—not just a worthy exercise to work off the *Apfelstrudel*.

Hiking. Don't be intimidated by a preconception of long, gruelling treks across steep, rough terrain. Hiking in the Tyrol is a relaxing, as well as exhilarating, pleasure. Routes up mountains, through forests and across meadows are clearly indicated with red or blue-and-

white markers. Detailed walking maps, available in resort tourist offices, specify the degree of difficulty of each route, indicating whether an itinerary is suitable for beginners or experienced, long-distance hikers. You can coordinate your excursion with postal bus service (see p. 124) if you don't want to limit yourself to circular tours. Many resorts provide guides for more ambitious tours, and some offer organized excursions, a good way of learning about local flora, fauna and folkways.

Rather than lugging a picnic, stop at one of the many waystations in farmhouses, known as *Jausenstationen* (literally "snack-station"), where you can get anything from apple juice, pastry and a sandwich to a hearty full meal. Dress sensibly. In summer, a beginner will not need hefty hiking boots, but you should have shoes with a sturdy rubber sole. If you're blister-prone, wear thin cotton socks under a second woollen pair to avoid rubbing. Bring along a sweater and anorak, even on the warmest day. You never know what's going on further up the mountain.

Mountain climbing. Take professional advice—and a guide, if you're a beginner. The facilities are first-class in every corner of this alpine land. Whatever is true about dress for hiking applies doubly to climbing. You can take climbing lessons in special schools in Innsbruck, Kitzbühel, Lienz, Mayrhofen, Alpbach, Reutte, Sölden—and many other resorts.

Bicycling. Bikes can be rented at most larger railway stations. It's a delightful way to see more of the country—for those who can handle hills.

Horse-riding. For this favourite Tyrolean pastime (riding is especially pleasant on forest paths), there are great facilities at Ebbser Fohlenhof in the Kaisergebirge (see p. 69), but also at Mayrhofen, Oberau, Kitzbühel and St. Johann, Seefeld and Reutte, etc.

Tennis. Courts of clay and other hard surfaces, indoors and out, abound in every resort, usually against an idyllic mountain backdrop that occasionally distracts your smash.

Golf. There are 18-hole golf courses in Innsbruck (Rinn) and Seefeld, 9 holes at Innsbruck (Sperberegg), Kitzbühel and Pertisau, and minigolf everywhere.

Water Sports. The alpine mud (*Moor,* they call it) insulating the lake bed keeps the water, even quite high in the mountains, delighfully warm for swimming. The best lakes for sailing and windsurfing are Plansee, Achensee and Walchensee. The more adventurous might like to try canoeing or rubber-rafting on the mountain torrents at Mayrhofen, in the Brandenberg Valley near Kramsach or on the Kössener Ache in the Kaisergebirge.

Winter Sports

Thanks to the great variety of valley formations, you can ski the Tyrol for years without repeating a run. But the region's major asset is the abundance of centuries-old villages that combine access to first-class skiing amenities with the attractions of traditional Tyrolean life.

For those who appreciate an active, sometimes even hectic, nightlife and the most professional skiing facilities Europe has to offer, there are Tyrol's big three: Kitzbühel, St. Anton and Seefeld. **Kitzbühel** is without doubt the most fashionable. Site of the mighty Hahnenkamm, it possesses more than 50 runs, ranging in difficulty from "greenhorn" to "hotshot". The *Skizirkus* (literally "ski circus") system provides a diversity of runs in the same area, such as the Ehrenbach (on the Hahnenkamm) or the Trattalm (on the Kitzbüheler Horn), so that skiers of different abilities can start off together. One of the great attractions for cross-country skiers is the nearly 2-mile (3 km.) nighttime run, lighted till 9.30 p.m.

St. Anton proves a great favourite of serious skier and fervent *après-ski* fan alike. The cradle of international professionals ever since Hannes Schneider introduced the Arlberg style in 1907, it still offers excellent facilities for beginners: 9 miles (15 km.) of downhill runs and 30 miles (47 km.) for cross-country enthusiasts, with free guides.

Seefeld has magnificent cross-country facilities, while providing first-rate downhill runs, too. The Seefeld Plateau linking Leutasch and Telfs takes you through beautiful mountain forests, 37 miles (60 km.) of paths immediately around Seefeld joining up with 62 miles (100 km.) more on the plateau.

Innsbruck is in a class by itself, combining the amenities of a large town with easy access to world-class skiing on the doorstep at Igls and Axams. Shuttle buses operate all day long to the cross-country runs in the Stubaital.

Mayrhofen in the Zillertal and **Serfaus-Fiss** in the Oberinntal have all the chic and professionalism of "Kitz" on a smaller, more intimate scale. Mayrhofen provides night-time cross-country skiing. Both resorts have excellent ski schools.

In the Lechtal, **Reutte's** Hahnenkamm offers fine family skiing. At the other end of the valley, **Elbigenalp** has a dozen runs in easy reach of an exquisite rustic setting.

Nestling in the Kaisergebirge and Kitzbühel Alps are a host of smaller, quieter resorts for those who don't relish Kitz's bustle: **St. Johann, Ellmau, Kössen** and **Walchsee** are among the best.

The glaciers of the Oetztal make **Sölden** a favourite target for both family skiers and rugged individualists. A cable car goes from the old village to the new hotel complex at Hochsölden and on up to the spectacular Gaislachkogel. The peak rises 10,030 feet (3,058 m.) above sea level.

East Tyrol is blessed with especially sunny winters in addition to abundant snow. Skiing here is more peaceful and easy-going than elsewhere in the Tyrol. Favourite resorts include **Sillian** in the Pustertal on the Italian frontier, **St. Jakob in Defereggen** and **Obertilliach** on the sunny side of the Lienzer Dolomites.

Fanatics can also pursue summer skiing on five southern oriented glaciers: the Zillertal's Hintertux, the Stubaital, the Oetztal and its side valley, the Kaunertal and the Pitztal. Cross-country skiing continues at high altitudes until April or May.

Tyrol has the world's most appealing cross-country runs.

Festivals and Folklore

The "Holy Land of Tyrol" seems to turn every religious holiday in the calendar into some sort of festival or procession, sometimes livened up by a good dose of pagan ritual, too.

Fastnacht (carnival) in February or March precedes the ascetic days of Lent, providing an excuse for dressing up in strange costumes and masks, getting tipsy and flirting with someone else's spouse. Easter in the Kaisergebirge is celebrated with Passion plays at Erl and Thiersee (not every year, check for dates); the whole community participates

in elaborate productions of the Crucifixion. On the Sunday after Easter, a colourful procession *(Virger Widderprozession)* takes place in the Virgental (East Tyrol). Villagers and a brass band wend their way from Virgen to the pilgrimage church at Obermauer (see p. 80), walking behind a ram festooned with flowers and ribbons in honour of the one ram in the valley that escaped a plague in the Middle Ages. All over the Tyrol people come out in their best costumes to dance around the maypole on May Day.

Corpus Christi Day *(Fronleichnam)* in June and Assumption *(Mariä Himmelfahrt)* in August are the most widely celebrated summer holy days. The Feast of St. John is especially spectacular in the Tyrolean Alps, where bonfires are set alight along the mountain ridges on Midsummer Night. At the end of August or beginning of September, you can see the picturesque *Almabtrieb*. Herders bring their cattle down from the mountain pastures for the winter, decorated with flowers and ribbons, led by the cow that has yielded the most milk. Each of these festivals is, of course, the pretext for parties in the local taverns, everybody welcome.

Folklore is a much-abused concept in the tourist business, and you cannot always be sure that the "Tyrolean Evening" offered in the big hotels has any real connection with authentic Tyrolean culture. Your best bet is to seek out a *Tiroler Abend* in one of the smaller villages, often in an unassuming little tavern where the beer and *Schnaps* flow fast, and if not free, at least not so expensive as in the towns.

The songs you'll hear are, naturally enough, hymns to good fellowship, sweet love and the joys of tending cattle in the alpine meadows—that's where the yodelling comes in. The dancing acts out the same themes. Watch, for instance, the flirtatious *Figurentanz* in which a boy in *Lederhose* dances around a girl in *Dirndl,* their arms interlacing in increasingly intricate configurations, peeping at each other over shoulders, under elbows—all very courtly—ending with the fellow on his knees before his lady. Or the *Schuhplattler,* with a lot of very noisy slapping and kicking. Like Tyrolean humour, these dances look

Tyroleans find a hundred excuses for holding village festivities.

knockabout and rough but don't actually hurt anyone—as you'll find out when you're invited to join in.

In the same rustic tradition, you can see peasant theatre (*Heimatbühne* or *Bauerntheater*) dedicated to broad farce, melodrama and touching romance in dozens of villages around the province. In Innsbruck, the Alt-Innsbrucker Bauerntheater und Ritterspiele gives performances in the Bierstindl tavern. Classical drama, opera and operettas are performed at Innsbruck's Tiroler Landestheater at Rennweg 2 and the Kammerspiele, around the corner at Universitätsstrasse 1.

Concerts of classical music and traditional folk music are held during the May spring festival *(Tiroler Frühling)* at Neustift in the Stubaital. Innsbruck features concerts at the Kongresshaus and Schloss Ambras, as well as chamber music and organ recitals in the Hofkirche and Basilika Wilten. All through the summer, brass bands and choirs perform in front of the capital's Goldenes Dachl and in the Hofgarten.

For a break from folklore, try your luck at roulette, blackjack or baccarat in the casinos at Kitzbühel or Seefeld.

Shopping

Like folklore, Tyrolean **craftwork** is not always easy to find in its authentic form, least of all at souvenir shops. Unless, of course, you have decided that the best way to handle the junk peddlers is to seek out their most outrageous dolls and glass snowballs, plastic saints, unsmokeable gnarled pipes and atrociously cuddly acrylic-fur animals and become a collector of the ultimate in super-kitsch.

But genuine pieces, distinguished by fine, traditional workmanship, are available. In Innsbruck, Tiroler Heimatwerk, Meranerstrasse 2, maintains a very high, carefully controlled standard. On sale are excellent examples of woodcarving, embroidery and weaving made in nearby Igls, Thaur and Absam. Or visit these villages yourself, watch the artisans at work and buy their products on the spot. The Lechtal is famous for handwoven carpets (visit the workshops at Stanzach), while glassware is the speciality of Rattenberg. In the workshops there you can watch craftsmen fashioning delicate ornaments or blowing ornate wine glasses and decanters.

As for **clothing,** Tyrolean costumes *(Trachten)* are something that usually look best on

Bolzano gets best of both worlds, Tyrol Speck *and Italian cheeses.*

Tyroleans. But for the children, you might like to buy *Lederhosen*—the leather shorts that last forever. (Don't clean them; as they get older and dirtier just rub off whatever cakes too thickly on them and stand them in the corner.) For yourself, the sturdy woollen *Loden* coats and jackets are now made in a range of bright colours, as well as traditional olive and grey. Long woollen socks are a real find in this land of outdoorsmen—often scarlet, if that's your taste, but all marvellously resistant to the cold and the wet. You'll also find a great selection of walking shoes and hiking boots.

Sports shops are, of course, stocked with the best **skiing** and **mountain-climbing equipment.**

Among gastronomic delights consider the **liqueurs** and *Schnaps* distilled in such areas as the Wildschönau. One delicacy that travels very well is the **Tiroler Speck,** superbly cured, smoked and spiced hams available in hermetically sealed packages. The more the rind looks like an old leather boot, the better it is. Once opened, if kept in a cool place, it will last for weeks.

Eating Out

The Tyrol is a simple, peasant place that serves simple peasant food. It's healthy robust fare, straightforward and unfussy but delicious. The restaurants are unpretentious—often, in the more isolated villages, quite simply the back room of a farmhouse.

The specialities that have evolved over the centuries are the result of making tasty, filling meals from frugal resources for a people tackling the daily rigours of mountain life. For the modern visitor, this means portions that are often too much to handle in two full meals each day. But nobody ever complains about being underfed*.

Meal Times

The local custom is to have a solid, hot midday meal, served from noon to 2 p.m.—rarely later, except in the mountains where you see the sign *Ganztägig warme Küche* (Hot meals all day long). A light supper of soup, cold meat, ham or sausage and perhaps a salad is served from about 7.00 to 9.00 p.m. (later in the larger towns). If your day's programme includes such strenuous outdoor activities as hiking or other sport, you may want to relieve a ravenous alpine appetite with a snack in mid-afternoon *(Jause)*.

Where to Eat

The inn (*Gasthof* or *Wirtshaus*) is without a doubt, next to the church, the most important institution in the life of Tyroleans. This is the social gathering place, where information and gossip are exchanged, political opinions formed and community solidarity reinforced. The local mayor is very often an inn-keeper. To get into the swing of village life, the Gasthof is the place to eat. Restaurants as such are a rarity outside the big towns. They are often attached to the more expensive hotels. Eat in a restaurant if you want a change from regional cooking—a Viennese meal, for example. But beware of places promising French cuisine; they're usually overpriced and mediocre. Anyway, why come to the Tyrol for a *blanquette de veau?* Even in Innsbruck, Kitzbühel or Kufstein, for instance, the atmosphere is more relaxed in the Gasthof.

Up in the mountains, the

* For a comprehensive guide to wining and dining in Austria, consult the Berlitz EUROPEAN MENU READER.

great eating establishment is the *Jausenstation.* Literally "snack stations", these alpine huts are dotted strategically across the landscape—heaven-sent oases saving hikers the trouble of carrying a picnic by offering lusty sustenance in a lovely setting. You can eat indoors if it's cold, but the ideal is to sit at outdoor tables on terraces commanding views of the valley you've just left or are about to descend into. You can have an open-face sandwich or a full meal from a limited but satisfying menu. The most ordinary food tastes like ambrosia up in the mountains. With luck, the Jausenstation is beside a stream from which they'll fish you a fresh trout.

In the towns, of course, there are also cafés *(Konditorei),* usually with open-air terraces, serving pastry in the grand Austrian tradition, as well as ice-cream, coffee, tea and fruit juices and a good selection of wines—plus light snacks, egg dishes and salads. And the hamburger and fried chicken fast-food chains have reached the Tyrol, too.

Breakfast

Tyroleans start the day with a meal that is somewhat more substantial than the typical Continental breakfast. The difference is the selection of cold meats—ham, salami and liver sausage—and cheese served with the bread rolls *(Semmel).* Coffee is stronger than German or Anglo-American brews, but weaker than French or Italian.

Soups and Starters

As elsewhere in Central Europe, soups are a regular feature of the meal. The choice includes *Bohnensuppe* (bean soup), often with pieces of sausage or bacon, and *Knödelsuppe* (dumpling soup), a chicken or beef broth with dumplings of flour, breadcrumbs, onions, bacon, parsley and garlic. Spicy *Gulaschsuppe,* inherited from Austro-Hungarian days, combines beef chunks, onions, garlic and paprika with tomatoes and heart of celery. A rarity awaits those of you really "going native": *Tiroler Mus,* a frugal but sustaining soup of semolina, enriched with butter.

The king of hors d'oeuvres is for many people the region's outstanding contribution to world cuisine, *Tiroler Bauernspeck.* This piquant, home-cured bacon is served raw, either in a chunk on a wooden board with a sharp knife to cut slices in your own preferred thickness, or sliced and arranged decoratively on a plate, sprinkled with a little horseradish. It's at its best aged to a dark, Burgundy red and cut to an almost transparent thinness. Connoisseurs unhesitatingly place it on a par with the aristocrats among hams and bacons of Parma, Bayonne, Prague, Westphalia or Virginia.

Beer is an ideal accompaniment to a hearty panful of Tiroler Gröstl.

Main Dishes

Perhaps the most popular local concoction is *Tiroler Gröstl,* a hearty dish of beef or pork sautéed with diced potatoes, chives, cumin and other herbs. It's served with a refreshing green cabbage salad. The variation known as *Herrngröstl* includes a fried egg.

Other pan-fried dishes *(Pfannengerichte)* guarantee a piping-hot meal, since they're usually served in the handle-less pan: *Bauernkotelett,* pork chops

sautéed with mixed vegetables, and *Spinatspätzle,* gnocchi-like spinach noodles sautéed with bacon and cream.

From Fügen to Mayrhofen, usually only at weekends, the better inns serve *Zillertaler Krapfen,* a sort of ravioli filled with grated potatoes, chives and sour cream. It's traditionally accompanied by a glass of buttermilk. The iron-stomached tackle *Beuschl,* the pungent local version of tripe. In season, *Rehkeule* and *Rehrücken* (venison) make a succulent but straightforward main course.

Most menus also include a couple of Viennese classics—*Wienerschnitzel,* a large, thinly sliced cutlet of veal (occasionally pork in these days of economic crunch), coated with egg and seasoned bread crumbs and crisply sautéed, and *Backhendl,* boned chicken prepared in the same way. These should be eaten with cold potato or cucumber salad.

Desserts

Tyroleans share the national taste for pastry. The variations of cherries, strawberries, hazelnuts, walnuts and apple in cakes *(Kuchen)* or pies and tarts *(Torten)* are endless. The best-known chocolate cake is Viennese *Sachertorte,* with a layer of apricot jam.

Hot desserts are popular, too. Try the Hungarian-style *Palatschinken,* wafer-thin pancakes filled with jam or nuts, and *Apfelstrudel,* thinly sliced apples with raisins and cinnamon rolled in an almost transparent flaky pastry. Or sweet dumplings with an apricot in the centre *(Marillenknödel),* or a plum *(Zwetschgenknödel).*

Drinks

The wine served in Tyrol is most often white, which Austrians drink quite happily with meat and fish alike. The only decent reds come from South Tyrol *(Kalterersee)* or Bad Vöslau, south of Vienna. The best-kown of Austrian white wines is the *Gumpoldskirchner,* full bodied, with a good bouquet. The Danube Valley produces wine with a light natural sparkle: the *Kremser, Dürnsteiner* and *Langenloiser.* To enjoy them at their best, order these wines dry *(herb),* as the producers often sweeten them for what they imagine to be foreign tastes.

Local beers are good, especially *Zillertaler,* but for old times' sake order the great Czechoslovak beer, *Pilsner Urquell,* readily available here. The regional *Schnaps* and liqueurs made from apricots, cherries, gentian and rowanberry *(Vogelbeere)* are heart-warming delights.

Natural, unadulterated fruit juices are excellent: honest-to-goodness apple *(Apfelsaft)* and grape *(Traubensaft).*

Cudgel Cake

If you're in the Brandenberg Valley (see p. 74), track down a speciality of the villages around Aschau or Brandenberg—the formidable cake known as *Prügeltorte.* Try to watch it being made—a complicated process requiring great skill. The cake is baked by turning it over a beech-wood fire on a long, slim cudgel-like log *(Prügel).* The log is wrapped in greaseproof paper around which successive layers of rich dough are applied, resulting in a long thick, slightly gnarled confection. A popular wedding or birthday present, the cake stands on end and lasts for weeks. Surprisingly, it never gets hard enough to serve as a real cudgel.

To Help You Order...

Could we have a table?	**Ich hätte gerne einen Tisch.**
Waiter!	**Herr Ober!**
I would like...	**Ich möchte gerne...**

Beer	**ein Bier**	Menu	**die Karte**
Bread	**etwas Brot**	Milk	**Milch**
Butter	**etwas Butter**	Mineral water	**Mineralwasser**
Cheese	**Käse**	Mustard	**etwas Senf**
Coffee	**einen Kaffee**	Potatoes	**Erdäpfel*/ Kartoffel**
Dessert	**Nachspeise**	Salad	**Salat**
Eggs	**Eier**	Salt	**Salz**
Fish	**Fisch**	Soup	**eine Suppe**
Fruit	**Obst**	Sugar	**Zucker**
Glass	**ein Glas**	Tea	**einen Tee**
Ice-cream	**Eis*/ Gefrorenes**	Vegetables	**Gemüse**
Lemon	**Zitrone**	Wine	**Wein**
Meat	**Fleisch**		

...and Read the Menu

Apfel	apple	**Knofel*/ Knoblauch**	garlic
Tafelspitz	boiled beef	**Kuchen**	cake
Birne	pear	**Lamm**	lamb
Erdbeeren	strawberries	**Nudeln**	noodles
Fisolen*/ Bohnen	green beans	**Obers*/Sahne**	cream
Forelle	trout	**Rindfleisch**	beef
Gekocht	boiled	**Rostbraten**	roast beef
Geröstetes	sautéed potatoes	**Salzburger Nockerl**	omelet soufflé
Geselchtes mit Kraut	smoked pork with sauerkraut	**Schinken**	ham
Hendl	chicken	**Schwammerl*/ Pilze**	mushrooms
Kalbfleisch	veal	**Schweinefleisch**	pork
Kalbshaxe	veal shank	**Torte**	layer cake
Kartoffelsalat	potato salad	**Wild**	game
Kirschen	cherries	**Wurst**	sausage
		Zwiebeln	onions

* Austrian term

How to Get There

From the British Isles

BY AIR: Munich international airport in Germany serves the Tyrol. In addition, connecting flights link London, Manchester and Dublin to Innsbruck via Zurich or Frankfurt.

Charter Flights and Package Tours. Numerous options are available, especially in winter for all-inclusive Tyrolean skiing holidays.

BY CAR: The quickest way to Innsbruck—"capital" of the Tyrol—is via Ostend, Brussels, Luxembourg, Stuttgart and Ulm. You can also put your car on a train from Brussels to Munich, a couple of hours' drive from Innsbruck.

BY TRAIN: From London, frequent express trains travel to Innsbruck by way of Zurich or Munich. The trip takes just under 24 hours.

From North America

BY AIR: Non-stop flights operate to Zurich, Frankfurt, Munich and Vienna from several North American cities. Continue to Innsbruck by air from Vienna, Zurich or Frankfurt. Or travel to the Tyrol by bus from Munich or Zurich.

Charter Flights and Package Tours. Various tour operators offer both individual and group packages to Austria, including skiing, hiking and sightseeing holidays in the Tyrol. Consult a travel agent for details of current programmes.

Note: If you wish to travel extensively on the Continent, buy a Eurailpass—a flat-rate, first-class train ticket valid in most of Western Europe for a specified time. The Eurail Youthpass provides those under age 26 with second-class travel.

Anyone under age 26 can purchase the Austria Ticket, good for unlimited travel on Austria's railways, postal buses, lake steamers and cable cars. The Inter-Rail Card, which must be purchased before leaving home, entitles Europeans under 26 and women over 60 and men over 65 to one month's unlimited second-class travel in almost 20 European countries.

When to Go

Whatever the season, the Tyrol reveals its charms. Go in winter for the skiing (the best months are January, February and March), in spring for alpine blossoms and high-altitude cross-country skiing, in summer and autumn for hiking, riding, tennis, fishing and mountain climbing. The temperature and hours of sunshine in the Tyrol depend largely on the altitude.

Average monthly (daytime) temperatures in Innsbruck:

	J	F	M	A	M	J	J	A	S	O	N	D
°C max.	1	4	11	15	20	23	25	24	21	15	7	2
min.	−6	−4	0	4	8	11	13	12	10	4	0	−4
°F max.	34	39	52	59	68	73	77	75	70	59	45	36
min.	21	25	32	39	46	52	55	54	50	39	32	25

Average monthly rainfall

	J	F	M	A	M	J	J	A	S	O	N	D
millimetres	54	49	41	52	73	110	134	108	81	67	53	46
inches	2	2	1½	2	3	4	5	4	3	2½	2	2

Planning Your Budget

To given you an idea of what to expect, here's a list of averge prices in Austrian schillings (S). They can only be approximate, however, as in Austria, too, inflation makes relentless inroads.

Accommodation. *Hotels* (double room with bath, per person per day), 5-star 800–1,500 S, 4-star 350–750 S, 3-star 250–500 S, 2-/1-star 150–300 S. *Farmhouses* (room with bath or shower and toilet) 100–170 S per person per day. Heating surcharge (winter) around 20 S per day (usually included in the rate). *Youth hostels* (bed, breakfast, linens) 80–120 S per night. *Camping* around 40–50 S per person, up to 40 S per car, up to 50 S per caravan (trailer), up to 40 S per tent.

Airport. Bus Munich–Kitzbühel 300 S, minibus (minimum 5 passengers) 420 S. Bus Zurich Airport–St. Anton (winter weekends) 350 S. Taxi Innsbruck airport–city centre 70 S.

Car hire (international company). *VW Golf C* 420 S per day, 4.20 S per km., 4,200 S per week with unlimited mileage. *BMW 316* 680 S per day, 6.80 S per km., 7,070 S per week with unlimited mileage. Add 21% VAT and contract charges plus 110–130 S per day collision damage waiver.

Entertainment. Cinema 55–120 S, disco 60–180 S (including one drink), Tyrolean evening 50–90 S.

Meals and drinks. Continental breakfast 40–80 S, lunch/dinner in fairly good restaurant 150–350 S, coffee 20–30 S, beer (½ l.) 20–30 S, Austrian wine (bottle) 100 –180 S, cocktail 40–90 S.

Mountain guides. 1,400 S per day plus 10% for each additional person in the party.

Skiing (major resorts, high season). Downhill packages, 1 week, half board 3,000–7,500 S per person. Cross-country skiing, half board 2,200–5,000 S per person per week. Equipment hire, downhill skis, sticks and boots, 50–130 S per day, cross-country 25–80 S. Group lessons, 1 day 300 S, 6 days 870 S. Private lessons, 1 hour 280 S plus 80 S for each additional person. Ski-lift pass, one day 180–300 S, 6 days 900–1,650 S (mostly around 1,000 S).

Transport. Train, Austria Ticket (up to 26 years of age, 16 days) 1,350 S, *Bundesnetzkarte* (Federal Railways network, 2nd class, 16 days) 1,960 S. Taxis 25 S plus 8.50 S per km. Trams and buses (Innsbruck) single ticket, 12 S, book of 5 tickets, 42.50 S, 10 tickets 82 S, 25 tickets 195 S.

BLUEPRINT for a Perfect Trip

An A-Z Summary of Practical Information and Facts

Contents

Listed after many entries is the appropriate German translation, usually in the singular, plus a number of phrases to help you when seeking assistance. Additional phrases and expressions are to be found on p. 125. A star (*) indicates relevant prices are to be found on p. 106.

A

ACCOMMODATION*. See also CAMPING and YOUTH HOSTELS. Thanks to a long tradition of inn-keeping, the Tyrol boasts a wide variety of accommodation ranging from modern, first class **hotels** and older palaces in the grand style to simple alpine establishments. Whatever your choice, it's essential to reserve well in advance, especially for the Christmas and Easter holidays and the peak summer months of July and August. But you needn't stay at a hotel.

Farmhouses *(Bauernhof).* A number of Tyrolean farmers offer hospitality to visitors, usually for stays of three days or more. There's never a dull moment, whether you help with the hay-making or simply use the farmhouse as a base for walking tours or fishing expeditions. Farmhouse holidays are economical and fun, especially for city children who don't know that milk comes from cows.

Mountain huts *(Schutzhütte).* These huts provide simple shelter (accommodation is generally dormitory-style) and perhaps a meal to the high-altitude tourist. Most of the huts belong to mountain-climbing or skiing associations. They are not hotels, and the guest is expected to help clean up and observe a certain code of behaviour and discipline. There are no facilities for the disposal of rubbish, so you'll have to carry yours away with you.

The Tyrolean Tourist Office distributes lists of hotels, campsites, holiday flats and farmhouses (see TOURIST INFORMATION). Note that the tourist office cannot make reservations; instead contact the accommodation desk at Innsbruck railway station, tel. (05222) 237 66.

an inn	**ein Gasthof**
a boarding house	**eine Pension**
a single/double room	**ein Einzel-/Doppelzimmer**
with/without bath (shower)	**mit/ohne Bad (Dusche)**
What's the rate per night?	**Was kostet eine Übernachtung?**

AIRPORT* *(Flughafen).* Munich international airport in Germany, the nearest to the Tyrol, lies about 85 miles (140 kilometres) from the heart of the region. Regular bus service operates from the terminal to the resort town of Kitzbühel. You will find banks, car hire desks, restaurants, coffee bars, news- and souvenir stands, a post office, hairdresser, hotel reservation desk, tourist information office and duty-free shop. Innsbruck airport handles internal flights, as well as those from Zurich, Frankfurt and other West German cities.

BICYCLE HIRE *(Fahrradverleih).* You can generally rent bikes by the hour or the day in major resorts and at railway stations. You can usually arrange to rent a bike at one station and return it to another. In some localities there are special trails for cyclists.

Are there bicycles for hire at this station?	**Kann man an diesem Bahnhof Fahrräder mieten?**
May I return it to another station?	**Kann ich es an einem anderen Bahnhof zurückgeben?**

CAMPING*. There are more than 80 sites in the Tyrol—beside lakes, in meadows or mountain areas, near towns. Facilities may include restaurants, grocery stores, children's swimming pools and supervised playgrounds. A dozen or so sites offer caravans for hire. Some sites are equipped for winter camping. The Tyrolean Tourist Office publishes a list of sites.

May we camp here?	**Dürfen wir hier zelten?**
Is there a campsite nearby?	**Gibt es in der Nähe einen Campingplatz?**
We have a tent/caravan (trailer).	**Wir haben ein Zelt/einen Wohnwagen.**

CAR HIRE* *(Autovermietung).* International car hire firms offer cheaper weekly rates to clients who book in advance. You can hire a car at airports and railway stations or from one of the local firms. Some companies allow you to hire the car in one town and return it to another. You have to be over 21 to rent a car, and you'll need a valid driving licence. Unless you pay by credit card, you'll have to leave a cash deposit.

I'd like to rent a car (for the day).	**Ich möchte (für heute) ein Auto mieten.**
for tomorrow	**für morgen**
for one day/for a week	**für einen Tag/für eine Woche**

CHILDREN. Most children of six or seven enjoy hiking and can manage a long walk—provided they stop along the way for a rest, drinks and snacks. More than 70 adventure playgrounds *(Waldspielplatz)* have been set up in forest areas where children can play in safety. And a number of resorts organize outings for children—nature walks, mushroom picking, picnics, punch and judy shows, pony rides, etc.

The Alpine Zoo at Weiherburg near Innsbruck is both educational and fun. Bus shuttle service operates on the hour from Maria-Theresien-Strasse.

Many resorts have multilingual kindergartens for children from three years old. Ski resorts operate nurseries *(Kindertageszentrum)* for skiing toddlers. There's also a nursery in Innsbruck at Pradlerplatz 6, tel. (05222) 452 82.

As for a baby-sitter, your hotel receptionist may be able to make arrangements. In Innsbruck, the university runs a student baby-sitting service, tel. (05222) 207 59. Elsewhere, contact the local tourist information office (see TOURIST INFORMATION).

Can you get me a baby-sitter for tonight?	**Können Sie mir für heute abend einen Babysitter besorgen?**

CIGARETTES, CIGARS, TOBACCO *(Zigaretten, Zigarren, Tabak).* All the usual cigarette brands and a wide range of cigars and tobacco are sold in specialized shops *(Tabak-Trafik),* as well as from vending machines. Local brands include Dames, Memphis and Flirt.

Smoking is prohibited in cinemas and theatres, on public transport and in the non-smoking sections of certain restaurants.

A packet of ...	**Eine Schachtel ...**
A box of matches, please.	**Eine Schachtel Streichhölzer (Zündhölzer), bitte.**

CLOTHING. Pack a few woollens with your summer clothes because evenings can be chilly in the mountains. A raincoat and spare pair of sunglasses may come in handy, while stout walking shoes and a waterproof cover-up, preferably with a hood, are essential for alpine rambles.

Many Austrians dress with relative formality (*i.e.* dark suits and cocktail dresses for opera, concerts and theatre in cities); in other respects, European norms apply. Dress respectfully when visiting churches. Casual dress is the rule in ski resorts. Non-slip boots may save you from injury on icy pavements in winter. If you're shopping for clothes or renting ski gear, the chart at right will help.

Men						
Clothing		Shirts		Shoes		
GB/USA	Aust.	GB/USA	Aust.	GB	USA	Aust.
34	44	14	36	7	7½	40
36	46	15	38	7½	8	41
38	48	16	40	8	8½	42
40	50	17	42	9	9½	43
42	52	17½	43	10	10½	44

Women								
Clothing			Shirts/Pullovers			Shoes		
GB	USA	Aust.	GB	USA	Aust.	GB	USA	Aust.
10	8	36	32	10	38			
12	10	38	34	12	40	4	5½	36
14	12	40	36	14	42	5	6½	37
16	14	42	38	16	44	6	7½	38
18	16	44	40	18	46	6½	8	38½
20	18	46	42	20	48	7	8½	39

COMMUNICATIONS

Post offices. Most branches keep regular post office hours (see HOURS), though Innsbruck's central post office at Maximilianstrasse 2 stays open round the clock. Stamps and information about postage rates are also available at tobacconists.

Telegrams. The minimum for a regular telegram is 7 words. Night-letters *(Brieftelegramm)* are transmitted like telegrams and delivered with the mail of the day. The cost per word is half that of a regular telegram (minimum 22 words).

Telephone. Public telephone booths can be recognized by the sign of a black receiver in a yellow circle and the word *Fernsprecher*. The booths post instructions in several languages. Note that you have to press a button for connection as soon as your party answers.

C

Reduced rates are in effect weekdays from 7 p.m. to 8 a.m. and from 1 p.m. Saturday to 8 a.m. Monday. Hotels impose a surcharge of at least 20% on long-distance calls.

Some useful numbers:

Directory information (Austria)	16
Operator for foreign area codes	08
Foreign operator	09

You'll find other important numbers on the first page of the telephone book. The front pages list area codes and telephone rates.

A stamp for this letter/postcard, please.	**Eine Briefmarke für diesen Brief/ diese Karte, bitte.**
express (special delivery)	**Eilzustellung**
airmail	**Luftpost**
registered	**Eingeschrieben**
Have you received any mail for ...?	**Ist Post da für ...?**
I want so send a telegram to ...	**Ich möchte ein Telegramm nach ... aufgeben.**
Can I use the telephone?	**Kann ich das Telefon benutzen?**
Can you get me this number in ...	**Können Sie mich mit dieser Nummer in ... verbinden?**
reverse-charge (collect) call	**R-Gespräch**
personal (person-to-person) call	**Gespräch mit Voranmeldung**

COMPLAINTS. Courtesy, calm and a touch of humour will invariably set your Tyrolean hosts running to put things right. But if charm fails and you remain dissatisfied, report the matter to the Tyrolean Tourist Office (see TOURIST INFORMATION). Generally a complaint in writing is more effective. For serious matters, contact the police or your consulate.

CONVERTER CHARTS. For tire pressure, see page 116. Austria uses the metric system.

Temperature

°C −30 −25 −20 −15 −10 −5 0 5 10 15 20 25 30 35 40 45
°F −20 −10 0 10 20 30 40 50 60 70 80 90 100 110

Length

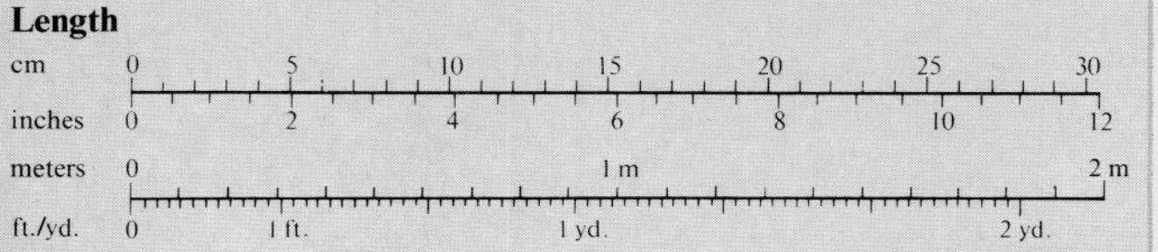

Weight

grams 0 100 200 300 400 500 600 700 800 900 1 kg

ounces 0 4 8 12 1 lb 20 24 28 2 lb.

Distance

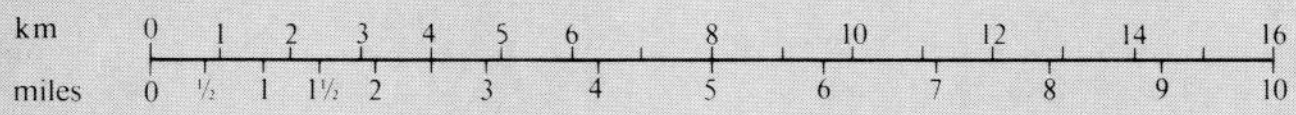

Fluid measures

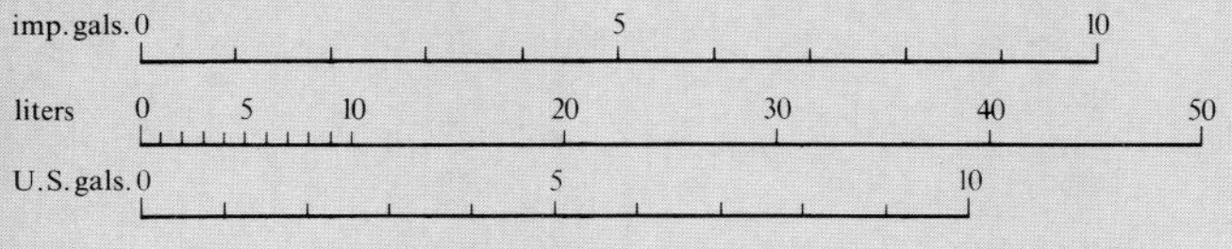

CRIME and THEFT. Austria's crime and theft rate is low. All the same, it is unwise to put temptation in the way of a potential thief by leaving your car unlocked or valuable objects on view inside. By the same token, do not leave money or valuables in your hotel room; store them in the safe instead. If you are robbed, report the incident to the nearest police station (see POLICE). If your passport is stolen, the police will give you a certificate to take to your consulate.

I want to report a theft.	**Ich möchte einen Diebstahl melden.**
My handbag/wallet has been stolen.	**Meine Handtasche/meine Brieftasche ist gestohlen worden.**

CUSTOMS *(Zoll)* and ENTRY REGULATIONS. To enter Austria, a valid passport is sufficient. Visitors from the United Kingdom need only show the British Visitor's identity card. But a visa is required for citizens of South Africa. Following are the items you can take into

Austria duty free (if you are over age 17) and then back into your own country.

Into:	Cigarettes	Cigars	Tobacco	Spirits	Wine
Austria 1)	200 or	50 or	250 g.	1 l. and	2 l.
2)	400 or	100 or	500 g.	1 l. and	2 l.
Australia	200 or	250 g. or	250 g.	1 l. or	1 l.
Canada	200 and	50 and	900 g.	1.1 l. or	1.1 l.
Eire	200 or	50 or	250 g.	1 l. and	2 l.
N. Zealand	200 or	50 or	½ lb.	1 qt. and	1 qt.
S. Africa	400 and	50 and	250 g.	1 l. and	1 l.
U.K.	200 or	50 or	250 g.	1 l. and	2 l.
U.S.A.	200 and	100 and	3)	1 l. or	1 l.

1) Arriving from European countries.
2) Arriving from non-European countries.
3) A reasonable quantity.

Tourists do not pay duty on items for personal use (jewellery, sports equipment, etc.), nor on gifts and souvenirs up to a value of 400 schillings.

Currency restrictions. There's no limit on the amount of foreign or Austrian currency you can bring into Austria, but you may take out no more than 15,000 schillings in Austrian currency without special permission.

VAT refunds. You'll be refunded the Value Added Tax *(Mehrwertsteuer)*, a sales tax, on purchases of more than 1,000 schillings per invoice if you take the goods out of the country without using them. Ask the salesperson to fill out a "U 34" form with your home address, passport number and the price. At the border ask customs officials to stamp the form. Then mail it back to the shop or to an office of the Austrian Automobile Club *(ÖAMTC)* for a refund by cheque or banker's order. If you are motoring, look out for an ÖAMTC office at the border for immediate reimbursement.

I've nothing to declare.	**Ich habe nichts zu verzollen.**
It's for my personal use.	**Das ist für meinen persönlichen Gebrauch.**

DRIVING IN AUSTRIA. To bring your car into Austria you will need:

- International driving licence (national licence for Europeans)
- Car registration papers
- Third party insurance (green card)
- National identity car sticker
- Red warning triangle in case of breakdown
- First-aid kit

Driving regulations: Drive on the right, overtake on the left. Rules of the road are similar to those in other European countries where traffic keeps to the right. Be sure to observe the following rules:

- fasten seat belts
- seat children under 12 in the back
- don't overtake on the right on motorways *(Autobahn)*
- give priority to vehicles coming from the right at crossroads and junctions, unless otherwise indicated
- give priority to trams
- never overtake a tram or bus which is slowing down or embarking or disembarking passengers
- don't use the horn in towns

Drunken driving is severely punished in Austria. The maximum permissible amount of alcohol in the blood is 0.8 per mille.

Alpine roads. Gradients of between 6 and 15% are common in the Alps. Caravans (trailers) are banned on certain routes. Vehicles must be equipped with snow tires, spikes or chains in snow conditions. Chains can be rented from the two Austrian automobile clubs, the ÖAMTC *(Österreichischer Automobil-, Motorrad- und Touring-Club)* and the ARBÖ *(Auto-, Motor- und Radfahrerbund Österreichs).* A bus or lorry (truck) going uphill has priority.

Breakdowns. Austrian automobile clubs offer 24-hour breakdown service to all drivers on motorways and main roads. For the ÖAMTC call (05222) 441 54 and for the ARBÖ (05222) 451 23.

Parking. There are five underground parking areas in Innsbruck. To park on the street in the city centre (maximum 90 minutes) you need a parking voucher sold in the city tourist office, tobacco kiosks and post offices. Some towns have blue zone parking; you display a disc, available free from kiosks, showing arrival and departure times.

Speed limits. The speed limit on motorways (expressways) is 130 kilometres per hour (80 mph); on other roads the limit is 100 kilometres per hour (60 mph). The maximum speed in towns is 50 kilometres per hour (35 mph). For cars towing a caravan or trailer weighing more than 750 kilos (1,650 lbs.) the speed limit on motorways is 70 kilometres per hour (45 mph), 60 kilometres per hour (40 mph) on other roads.

Tolls. A number of Tyrolean roads and tunnels charge tolls, notably the Brenner and Tauern motorways, the Grossglockner Alpine road and the Arlberg tunnel.

Tire Pressure

lb./sq. in.	kg/cm²	lb./sq. in.	kg/cm²
10	0.7	26	1.8
12	0.8	27	1.9
15	1.1	28	2.0
18	1.3	30	2.1
20	1.4	33	2.3
21	1.5	36	2.5
23	1.6	38	2.7
24	1.7	40	2.8

Road signs. Most road signs used in Austria are international pictographs, but here are some written signs you might come across.

Anfang	(Parking) Start
Ausfahrt	Exit
Aussicht	Viewpoint
Bauarbeiten	Road works
Einbahn	One way
Ende	(Parking) End
Fahrbahnwechsel	Change lanes
Fußgänger	Pedestrians
Gefährlich	Danger
Geradeaus	Straight on
Glatteis	Slippery road
Halten verboten	No stopping
Licht einschalten	Use headlights
Ortsende	Town ends
Parken erlaubt	Parking allowed
Rechts, links einbiegen	Turn rights left
Rollsplitt	Loose gravel
Sackgasse	Dead end street
Spital	Hospital
Steinschlag	Falling stones
Umleitung	Diversion (detour)
Vorfahrt	Priority
Vorsicht	Caution
Werktags von 7 bis 17 Uhr	Weekdays 7 a.m. to 5 p.m.
Zufahrt gestattet	Entry permitted

driving licence	**Führerschein**
car registration papers	**Zulassungsschein**
green card	**Grüne Karte**

Where's the nearest car park?	**Wo ist der nächste Parkplatz?**
Can I park here?	**Kann ich hier parken?**
Are we on the right road for ...?	**Sind wir auf der richtigen Strasse nach ...?**
Full tank, please.	**Bitte volltanken.**
Check the oil/tires/battery, please.	**Öl/Reifen/Batterie prüfen, bitte.**
I've had a breakdown.	**Ich habe eine Panne.**
There's been an accident.	**Es ist ein Unfall passiert.**

ELECTRIC CURRENT. Austria's standard voltage is 220-volt, 50-cycle A.C. Check your appliances to see whether a plug adaptor or transformer will be required.

an adaptor/a battery	**ein Zwischenstecker/eine Batterie**

EMBASSIES and CONSULATES *(Botschaft; Konsulat).* Most consulates and all embassies are in Vienna. Here's a list of addresses.

Australia:	Mattiellistrasse 2–4, 1040 Vienna, tel. (0222) 52 85 80
Canada:	Dr. Karl-Lueger-Ring 10, 1010 Vienna, tel. (0222) 63 36 91
Eire:	Hilton Center, Postfach 1039, 1030 Vienna, tel. (0222) 75 42 46
New Zealand:	Hollandstrasse 2, 1030 Vienna, tel. 26 44 81
South Africa:	Sandgasse 33, 1190 Vienna, tel. (0222) 32 64 93
United Kingdom:	Reisnerstrasse 40, 1030 Vienna, tel. (0222) 73 15 75
U.S.A.:	Boltzmanngasse 16, 1090 Vienna, tel. (0222) 34 66 11

EMERGENCIES. Emergency numbers are listed at the front of the telephone book. Here are the most important ones.

Ambulance	144
Police	133
Fire	122
Mountain Rescue	194
Medical Service	(05222) 355 44

I need a doctor/dentist.	**Ich brauche einen Arzt/ Zahnarzt.**

G

GUIDES*. Although there are more than 350 mountain and ski guides in the Tyrol, it can be difficult to find a qualified guide—whether for cross-country skiing tours in April and May or during the peak of the mountaineering period (July and August). It is best to arrange for a guide in advance by writing to the Tyrolean Mountain and Ski Guide Association:

Tiroler Berg- und Schiführer Verband, Postfach, 6010 Innsbruck, tel. (05222) 361 30/353 40.

The Tyrolean Tourist Office (see TOURIST INFORMATION) also publishes lists of guides.

We'd like an English-speaking guide/mountain guide.	**Wir möchten einen englischsprachigen Fremdenführer/ Bergführer.**
What is the fee per hour/day?	**Was kostet es pro Stunde/Tag?**

H

HAIRDRESSERS *(Friseur).* It's wise to telephone for an appointment at a woman's hairdressers *(Damenfriseur).* There are several in Innsbruck and one or two in all but the smallest Tyrolean villages.

Not too much off (here).	**(Hier) nicht zu kurz schneiden.**
A little more off (here).	**(Hier) ein wenig kürzer schneiden.**
a colour chart	**eine Farbtafel**
a colour rinse	**eine Farbspülung**
a blow-dry	**Föntrocknen**
a shampoo and set	**Waschen und Legen**
a haircut	**ein Haarschnitt**

HOURS. Most shops are open from 8.30 a.m. to 6 p.m., though the smaller establishments close for a couple of hours for lunch. On Saturday shops close at noon or 1 p.m.

Chemists (pharmacies) open during normal business hours, as well as in turns at weekends and at night. After hours, shops usually display the address of the nearest chemists open.

Banks do business Monday to Friday from 7.45 a.m. to 12.30 p.m. and from 2.30 to 4 p.m. On Thursday they stay open until 5.30 p.m.

Post offices are open Monday to Friday from 8 a.m. to noon and 2 to 5 or 6 p.m. Branches in railway stations may open round the clock, including Sundays and public holidays. In most resorts, post offices also open on Saturday from 8 to 10 a.m.

LANGUAGE. Austria is German-speaking, but English is widely understood. If you don't speak German, start off a conversation with a polite *Sprechen Sie Englisch?* (Do you speak English?). When you meet people in a lift or enter a shop say *Guten Tag* (Good Day) or *Guten Abend* (Good Evening). On leaving say *Auf Wiedersehen* (Good-bye). Young people prefer *Servus* or *Pfiati* ("Bye" or "See you soon"), to the more formal *Auf Wiedersehen*. For their part, Tyroleans generally hail each other with a *Grüss Gott* (God greet you).

The Berlitz phrase book GERMAN FOR TRAVELLERS covers most of the situations you are likely to encounter in Austria, and the German-English/English-German pocket dictionary contains a special menu-reader supplement.

L

LAUNDRY and DRY-CLEANING. Town or village dry-cleaners and launderettes generally prove cheaper than hotel service, and sometimes just as quick. Look in the yellow pages under *Wäschereien* (laundries) and *Putzereien* (dry-cleaners). Innsbruck's launderette at Amraser Strasse 15 is open Monday to Friday from 7.45 a.m. to 6 p.m.

When will it be ready?	**Wann ist es fertig?**
For tomorrow morning please.	**Bis morgen früh, bitte.**

LOST PROPERTY. If you leave something in a train, contact the central collecting office for the Austrian Federal Railways:
Zentralsammelstelle der Österreichischen Bundesbahnen, Langauergasse 2, Westbahnhof, Vienna, tel. (0222) 56 50 29 96.

In Innsbruck, contact police headquarters:
Bundespolizeidirektion, Kaiserjägerstrasse 7, tel. (05222) 267 21.

Elsewhere, get in touch with the local police station.

I've lost may passport/wallet/ handbag.	**Ich habe meinen Pass/meine Brieftasche/meine Handtasche verloren.**

M

MAPS. Excellent free maps of Innsbruck and other towns are available at the tourist offices, most banks, car hire firms and bigger hotels. Falk-Verlag, Hamburg, who prepared the maps for this book, publish a detailed map of Austria.

The tourist offices distribute special maps for hikers. The Kompass series of walking maps includes maps of the Kaisergebirge, Lechtaler

Alps, Achensee and Rofangebirge, Innsbruck and Brenner, plus many other popular resort areas in the Tyrol.

I'd like a street plan of Innsbruck.	**Ich möchte einen Stadtplan von Innsbruck.**
a road map/hiking map of this region	**eine Strassenkarte/Wanderkarte dieser Gegend**

MEETING PEOPLE. Village inns *(Gasthof* or *Wirtshaus)* serve as unofficial community social centres where strangers and locals alike get together. You'll also see lots of local people out on the hiking trails and on the ski runs, especially at weekends and during holidays. Wish them "Grüss Gott" and you'll probably fall into conversation, for the Tyrol is relaxed, casual, friendly, an ideal place to make new friends.

MEDICAL CARE *(Ärztliche Hilfe).* See also EMERGENCIES. Make sure that your insurance policy covers medical treatment in Austria, particularly if you intend to go climbing or to indulge in winter sports. Even a minor injury can involve an expensive evacuation, sometimes by helicopter.

Chemists *(Apotheke)* are open Monday to Friday and on Saturday mornings (see HOURS). After hours, they display the address of the nearest shop on duty. Telephone (05222) 27073 to find out which chemists are open.

MONEY MATTERS. See also PLANNING YOUR BUDGET, p. 106. Austria's monetary unit is the *Schilling,* abbreviated *S, ÖS,* or *Sch.* It's divided into 100 *Groschen* (abbreviated *g.*). There are coins of 1, 5, 10 and 20 schillings and 2, 5, 10 and 50 groschen. Don't confuse the similar 5- and 10-schilling pieces. Banknotes are found in denominations of 20, 50, 100, 500 and 1,000 schillings.

Banks and currency exchange *(Bank; Wechselstube).* Foreign currency can be changed in practically all banks and savings banks *(Sparkasse).* Travel agencies and hotels also change money, but the rate may not be as good. The currency exchange desk at Innsbruck's city tourist office *(Städtisches Verkehrsbüro)* in Burggraben 3 is open Monday to Friday from 8 a.m. to noon and from 2 to 5.30 p.m., Saturday from 9 a.m. to noon. You can also change money at Innsbruck's central railway station daily from 7.30 a.m. to 8.30 p.m.

Credit cards, traveller's cheques, eurocheques. Traveller's cheques are welcome almost everywhere, and most major hotels and many restaurants and shops accept credit cards. Eurocheques are widely used in Austria.

I want to change some pounds/ dollars.	**Ich möchte Pfund/Dollars wechseln.**
Do you accept traveller's cheques?	**Nehmen Sie Reiseschecks?**
Can I pay with this credit card?	**Kann ich mit dieser Kreditkarte zahlen?**

PETS. You are allowed to bring up to two animals (cats or dogs) into Austria provided they have valid anti-rabies vaccination certificates with an authorized German translation.

PHOTOGRAPHY. Many museums allow you to take pictures (sometimes for a small fee), but never with a tripod or flash. If you plan to take pictures at high altitudes, ask your camera dealer for advice about special lens filters.

I'd like a film for this camera.	**Ich möchte einen Film für diese Kamera.**
a black-and-white film	**ein Schwarzweissfilm**
a film for colour prints	**ein Farbfilm**
a colour-slide film	**ein Diafilm**
a 35-mm film	**ein Fünfunddreissig-Millimeter-Film**
a super-8 film	**ein Super-acht-Film**
How long will it take for this film to be developed?	**Wie lange dauert es, diesen Film zu entwickeln?**
May I take a picture?	**Darf ich ein Foto machen?**

POLICE *(Polizei).* The police in the Tyrol generally keep a low profile. In cities, women manage traffic and hand out parking tickets. If you are fined for any reason, the police have the right to ask you to pay on the spot. Look under *Bezirkspolizeikommissariat* in the telephone book for the number of the local district police station. The emergency number for police is 133.

Where is the nearest police station?	**Wo ist die nächste Polizei-Wachstube?**

PUBLIC HOLIDAYS *(Feiertag).* Austria observes 14 public holidays a year during which banks and many restaurants are closed and official services suspended.

P

January 1	*Neujahrstag*	New Year's Day
January 6	*Heilige Drei Könige*	Twelfth Night
May 1	*Tag der Arbeit*	Labour Day
August 15	*Mariä Himmelfahrt*	Assumption
October 26	*Nationalfeiertag (Tag der Fahne)*	National Holiday (Flag Day)
November 1	*Allerheiligen*	All Saints' Day
December 8	*Unbefleckte Empfängnis*	Immaculate Conception
December 25	*Weihnachten*	Christmas Day
December 26	*Stefanstag*	St. Stephen's Day
Movable dates:	*Karfreitag*	Good Friday
	Ostermontag	Easter Monday
	Christi Himmelfahrt	Ascension Day
	Pfingstmontag	Whit Monday
	Fronleichnam	Corpus Christi

Are you open tomorrow? **Haben Sie morgen geöffnet?**

R

RELIGIOUS SERVICES *(Gottesdienst).* The Tyrol is strongly Roman Catholic, but a few other denominations and faiths hold services. Mass in big churches or cathedrals is often accompanied by orchestral and choral works. Processions, singing and performances of music occur during religious holidays. Mass is celebrated in English every Saturday in the crypt of the Jesuit Church, Universitätstrasse, Innsbruck.

A Protestant service takes place Sundays at the Holiday Inn Hotel, Salurner Strasse 15, Innsbruck.

S

SKIING*. Many Tyrolean resorts offer visitors guest cards good for free transport from town centres to runs and lifts and for reductions on cable cars and chair lifts, as well as on admission charges to indoor swimming pools, saunas, solariums, museums and attractions, depending on locality. Multiple lift tickets can be purchased in the form of coupons or a book *(Punktekarte* or *Block);* a pass allows unlimited use for a specified period, usually from three to 15 days.

For recorded information about general snow conditions, telephone (05222) 192. Or ring the Tyrolean Tourist Office Monday to Friday from 8 a.m. to noon and 2 to 5 p.m., (05222) 20 777.

TIME DIFFERENCES. Austria follows Central European Time (GMT + 1). In Summer, when clocks move ahead one hour to GMT + 2, the time difference looks like this:

New York	London	**Tyrol**	Jo'burg	Sydney	Auckland
6 a.m.	11 a.m.	**noon**	noon	8 p.m.	10 p.m.

TIPPING. A service charge is included in hotel and restaurant bills, so tipping is not obligatory. However, it is appropriate to give something extra to porters, cloakroom attendants and others who are of service to you. The chart below indicates how much to leave.

Porter, per bag	10 S
Maid, per week	50 S
Waiter	5% (optional)
Lavatory attendant	5–10 S
Taxi driver	10%
Guide	10%
Barber/Hairdresser	10–15%

TOILETS. Public facilities can be found in railway stations and near main squares of large towns, often in the pedestrian subways (underpasses). Normally toilets in cafés can be used without ordering anything, but it's more courteous to have a coffee or a beer.

You may have to pay a fee to use soap and towels. Have a couple of schillings ready in case the door has a slot.

Toilets may be labelled with symbols of a man and a woman, the initials W.C. or with *Damen* (Ladies) and *Herren* (Gentlemen).

Where are the toilets? **Wo sind die Toiletten?**

TOURIST INFORMATION. The Austrian National Tourist Office *(Österreichische Fremdenverkehrswerbung)* provides information about what to see, where to go and where to stay in the Tyrol. Its representatives abroad (see list below) are friendly and efficient. Note that the tourist office is a non-commercial organization and as such cannot make reservations.

Australia:	A.N.T.O., 19th floor, 1 York Street, Sydney 2000, NSW, tel. 27 85 81.
Canada:	A.N.T.O., 401 Bay Street/Suite 2008, Box 21, Toronto, Ontario M5H 2Y4, tel. 363 3677.
Eire:	A.N.T.O., The Lodge, Ardoyne House, Pembroke Park, Ballsbridge, Dublin 4, tel. 68 33 21.
South Africa:	A.N.T.O., Trust Bank Centre, Eloff Street, Johannesburg 2001, tel. 21 11 37.
United Kingdom:	A.N.T.O., 30 St. George's Street, London W1R 9FA, tel. (01) 629 0461.
U.S.A.:	A.N.T.O., 500 Fifth Avenue, Suite 2009–2022, New York, NY 10110, tel. (212) 697-0651. A.N.T.O., 3440 Wilshire Blvd., Los Angeles, CA 90010, tel. (213) 380-3309. A.N.T.O., 4800 San Felipe Street, Suite 500, Houston, TX 77056, tel. (713) 850-8888.

You may also want to get in touch with one of the following:

Tyrolean Tourist Office *(Tiroler Fremdenverkehrswerbung),* Bozner Platz 6, A-6010 Innsbruck, tel. (05222) 20 777.

South Tyrol Tourist Bureau, Piazza Walther 22, Bolzano, Italy, tel. (040471) 269 91.

Salzburg Tourist Bureau, Mozartplatz 1, Salzburg, tel. (06 22) 415 61.

For information about mountain climbing, hiking, mountain huts, glacier tours, ski resorts, winter sports, etc., contact the Austrian Alpine Association *(Österreichischer Alpenverein),* Wilhelm-Greil-Strasse 15, A-6020 Innsbruck, tel. (05222) 241 06.

TRANSPORT

Taxis*. Metered taxis serve larger towns; otherwise fixed rates apply. For long-distance trips, agree on the fare in advance.

Postal bus *(Postautobus).* These bright yellow conveyances serve even the smallest villages. Timetables are available from the Post Office Traffic Office *(Postverkehrsbüro)* in major towns. Buy tickets at the bus station or on the bus itself. If you intend to use the system

T

extensively, inquire about weekly tickets for unlimited travel in certain regions.

Mountain railways, cable cars and chair lifts carry passengers to heights of over 9,500 feet (3,000 metres).

Steamers ply the larger lakes from May to September.

Trains* *(Zug).* Austrian Federal Railways *(ÖBB)* trains link Innsbruck to other Austrian towns as well as to Munich, Zurich and Milan. Purchase tickets and make reservations at railway stations or travel agencies. Look out for special reductions including the Austria Ticket, the Junior Austria Ticket and rail passes for individual provinces. Children under six travel free. The following table gives a description of the trains that operate in Austria.

<table>
<tr><td>Expresszug
Schnellzug</td><td colspan="2">The fastest trains</td></tr>
<tr><td>Städteschnellzug</td><td colspan="2">Frequent intercity trains connecting the biggest towns</td></tr>
<tr><td>Eilzug</td><td colspan="2">Through trains, stop at main towns</td></tr>
<tr><td>Personenzug</td><td colspan="2">Local trains, stop at almost every station</td></tr>
<tr><td>Schlafwagen
Sleeping-car with 1-, 2- or 3-bed compartments including washing facilities.</td><td>Speisewagen
Dining-car</td><td>Liegewagen
Car containing 6-berth compartments (couchette) with bed linen.</td></tr>
</table>

When's the next bus/train to ...?	**Wann fährt der nächste Bus/Zug nach ...?**
I want a ticket to ...	**Ich möchte eine Fahrkarte nach ...**
single (one-way)	**einfach**
return (round-trip)	**hin und zurück**
first/second class	**erste/zweite Klasse**

WATER *(Wasser).* Fresh and clean, Tyrolean water tastes as if it came straight from a mountain stream—and probably did. Signs saying *Kein Trinkwasser* mean the water's not fit to drink.

YOUTH HOSTELS* *(Jugendherberge).* To stay in the Tyrol's youth hostels, you'll need an international membership card, preferably from your national youth hostel association. On the spot, youth hostel cards and information can be obtained at the young people's waiting room, Innsbruck central railway station, or from the Tyrolean section of the Austrian Youth Hostel Association, Südtiroler Platz 14–16, Innsbruck, tel. (05222) 277 71.

SOME USEFUL EXPRESSIONS

yes/no	**ja/nein**
please/thank you	**bitte/danke**
excuse me/you're welcome	**Entschuldigung/gern geschehen**
how long/how far	**wie lange/wie weit**
where/when/how	**wo/wann/wie**
yesterday/today/tomorrow	**gestern/heute/morgen**
day/week/month/year	**Tag/Woche/Monat/Jahr**
left/right	**links/rechts**
big/small	**gross/klein**
cheap/expensive	**billig/teuer**
open/closed	**offen/geschlossen**
hot/cold	**heiss/kalt**
old/new	**alt/neu**
I don't understand.	**Ich verstehe nicht.**
Please write it down.	**Schreiben Sie es bitte auf.**
What does this mean?	**Was heisst das?**
I'd like ...	**Ich hätte gern ...**
How much is that?	**Wieviel kostet das?**
Please help me.	**Bitte helfen Sie mir.**
Fetch a doctor—quickly!	**Holen Sie einen Arzt – schnell!**
Waiter/waitress (please).	**Herr Ober/Fräulein (bitte).**

DAYS OF THE WEEK

Sunday	**Sonntag**	Thursday	**Donnerstag**
Monday	**Montag**	Friday	**Freitag**
Tuesday	**Dienstag**	Saturday	**Samstag**
Wednesday	**Mittwoch**		

Index

An asterisk (*) next to a page number indicates a map reference. Where there is more than one set of page references, the one in bold type refers to the main entry. For index to Practical Information, see p. 107.

028/503 SUD